C000277510

The SAILOR'S BLUFFING *Bible*

For Kate

The SAILOR'S BLUFFING Bible

Make your mark in the sailing world

Tim Davison

Illustrated by John Quirk

FERNHURST

BOOKS

Published in 2021 by Fernhurst Books Limited
© 2021 Fernhurst Books Limited
The Windmill, Mill Lane, Harbury, Leamington Spa, Warwickshire.
CV33 9HP, UK
Tel: +44 (0) 1926 337488 | www.fernhurstbooks.com

This publication is designed to provide accurate and authoritative
information in regard to bluffing about sailing. However, the reader
should acknowledge that when bluffing there is a personal skill factor
(PSF) that they may not possess, and they may turn out to be terrible at
it, despite all the excellent advice given in this scholarly publication. The
Publisher accepts no responsibility for any errors or omissions, or for any
accidents or mishaps which may arise from the use of this publication.

Illustrations © John Quirk

Thanks and acknowledgements to the Arthur Ransome Literary Estate
for permission to use extracts from the author's writings.

A catalogue record for this book is available from the British Library
ISBN 978-1-912621-39-2

Designed by Daniel Stephen
Printed in Bulgaria by Multiprint

CONTENTS

INTRODUCTION

Must I go down to the sea again?

These days it's everywhere – in photos, adverts, on TV after the watershed, available for free on the web. Yes, sailing is never far from our thoughts, and apparently some men fantasise every 20 seconds about owning a boat.

And why not? There's nothing like cruising downwind in the sun, a glass of something passable in your hand, Springsteen's *Born to Run* at full blast on the cockpit speakers, and an adoring companion by your side.

Unfortunately sailing is nothing like that, and you're more likely to finish up cold, wet, seasick and penniless. And you'll probably spend the evening fixing the cockpit speakers, knackered by years of salt spray.

But that's only if you're foolhardy enough to actually go sailing. The trick is, of course, to stay ashore and bluff your fellow matelots into believing that you would be out there but for the gangrene you still have from the Atlantic crossing / your oilskins still being repaired after the 360 degree capsize / the foundry still casting your new Titanium winged keel.

Indeed, sailing is such a complex sport it begs for bluffing on an industrial scale. Luckily nobody knows everything about wind, weather, navigation, collision regulations, anchoring, maintenance, sails and so on, though this book aims to give you just enough knowledge to sit in the bar and bluff in most of these areas. You simply need to find out where your audience is least knowledgeable, then concentrate your bluffing skills on that.

Start with bland statements and queries that won't reveal your ignorance. 'Bit of a blow forecast for tomorrow. Does it get dodgy here when it comes from the north-east?' If someone turns out to be a meteorologist, quickly move on to the Racing Rules. 'We were on starboard tack and he hit us on the port quarter. Of course, we protested under Rule 42.2 (a) Subsection 1, and I'm pretty sure the Protest Committee will chuck him out under that, or even for bringing the sport into disrepute...'

No one will have the faintest idea what you're talking about, and neither will you, but you should now be set to bask in the warm glow of their admiration – or at least not be rumbled as a bluffer.

You get the idea. Armed with the essential sailing insights and key jargon contained within this precious volume, you should be accepted in the sailing club or in the cockpit as a passable sailor, man or woman[1]. Never again will you confuse a Pan Pan with a marine toilet, or a painter with someone who paints, and you'll always give the firm impression that you fully understand the importance of jib luff tension.

---

[1] Gender matters, but sailing can be a sport of few words, especially in a Force 7 blow. It is in this spirit of economy, and not out of any gender bias, that we have employed the shorter and simpler forms 'he', 'him' and 'man' in preference to the longer 'he and / or she', 'him and / or her' and 'man and / or woman'. As any bluffer will tell you, egalitarianism is alive and well on the high seas. Though not necessarily in the clubhouse...

Chapter 1

BEATING & RUNNING

This chapter is not about public school life, but the way a boat sails – which is central to successful bluffing about the theory and practice of sailing. You might think it's unnecessary to know any nautical science, but a bluffer will inevitably get drawn into technical conversations. So it's as well to be prepared. And, as a plus, understanding what's going on may help you avoid some of the hairier cock-ups waiting for you afloat.

Wind

Wind is a sailing boat's driving force. The moving air pushes on the sail and the sail pushes the boat along.

So far so good. The only problem is you can't see the wind.

Wind has two characteristics, strength and direction.

Strength is easy – you can feel a gentle wind on your cheek, a stronger breeze ruffles your hair and a gale blows your hat off. Sailors measure the wind in knots (roughly, miles per hour) and on the Beaufort Scale. As a bluffer just remember that a good wind for sailing is from 7-16 knots (Force 3-4). Anything over 22 knots (Force 6) is going to be hairy.

Force 6 wind blows the head off beer

For bluffing gold you can drop casually into the conversation that 'The force of the wind on a sail is proportional to the square of the windspeed (because there are more molecules hitting the sail and they're going faster). Thus, if the wind increases from 10 knots to 12 knots (which isn't much) the force goes from 100 units to 144 units, a 44% increase.' Pause to receive admiring looks from your newfound sailing friends, then apologise for getting technical and·decline to go further. In their eyes you have, hopefully, proved beyond doubt that you are a bona fide expert.

Wind direction is harder to pin down, though there are clues everywhere. A seagull always stands with its beak pointing into the wind, so its feathers aren't ruffled. The arrow on a weathercock points into the wind. A feather on a lake is blown downwind. Waves on the sea travel downwind, and so on.

On a boat it's helpful to have a burgee (flag) at the top of the mast to show the crew which way the wind is blowing. It's important to note that the free edge of the cloth points *downwind*. The wind is coming from the opposite direction, i.e. from *upwind*. Quite clear on this?

Gone with the wind

By this stage you may be beginning to wonder if there *is* any point to sailing. And the answer is 'yes', because you can (with a bit of skill) get the boat to sail in any direction you like – away from the wind, across it or even towards it.

Running is where the crew let out the sails and the boat moves away from the wind, blowing along like the feather on a pond mentioned above. The boat is level, and the crew can strip down to their swimsuits and enjoy the sun. But now the skipper decides to alter course 90 degrees towards the wind.

Reaching (not to be confused with retching, of which more later) is where the boat sails across the wind. The sails are pulled halfway in, the boat heels to the breeze and the speed picks up.

Now the gormless skipper decides to alter course again, turning a further 45 degrees towards the wind.

Beating is what the boat is doing now. The sails are pulled right in and, in a dinghy, the centreboard is pushed right down. The effect is like squeezing a piece of soap between thumb and forefinger – the wind is the thumb, and the resistance of the keel / centreboard is the forefinger. In the first case the soap shoots forward and in the second the boat does the same.

If you try to turn further into the wind the sails simply flap (they are already pulled right in) and the boat stops. So if you want to sail to a destination upwind you have to sail a zigzag course to windward (facing the wind). At the end of each zig (or zag) the boat turns through 90-odd degrees, and this turn is called 'a tack'.

Because you're going into the wind it's cooler and there's a lot more spray, so the crew reluctantly put their clothes back on. The boat also heels even more than it did on the reach.

Heeling in a yacht can be quite alarming if you're not used to it, so hang on to something solid. The bluffer might slip into the conversation that 'There's no need to panic – the heeling effect of the wind on the sails *decreases* as the boat heels further, while the righting effect of the keel *increases*. Eventually the two balance and the boat sails ahead at a steady angle. In fact, in theory, the wind can't capsize a yacht, though huge waves can.' Hopefully your audience will be reassured and won't notice your white knuckles (thank goodness oilskins have long sleeves).

Hang on to something solid

Dinghies can heel too but are designed to be sailed upright. Since these boats don't have a heavy keel, the crew provide the righting effect by moving their weight to the windward deck and sitting out (leaning back), with their toes under the toestraps. This effect can be magnified by use of a trapeze, of which more later. The good news is that if you are of generous proportions your bulk will be in demand for once, especially in a blow. So you *can* keep eating all the pies…

Steer clear

The safest, driest and simplest place on a yacht is at the helm (steering). It is essential that the bluffer moves aft (back) to this position as soon as possible. At the skipper's briefing jobs will be allocated, so you might mention that you used to love foredeck evolutions / navigating / grinding winches / cooking but sadly because of your dodgy knee you have been doing a lot of helming recently and would love to 'see how she goes.'

Surprisingly, the skipper may well take you up on this. He is probably the only person who knows how to do the other jobs and will be glad to be freed up to show the rest of the crew the ropes. It's amazing that the most incompetent person on a yacht worth half a million quid often finishes up steering her while the skipper is on the foredeck sorting out problems with the spinnaker, anchor, etc., but it happens all the time.

Your boat may be steered by a wheel or a tiller. A wheel is easy to use – it's just like steering a car. Since you're at the back end of the boat and might fall off, it's best to wear a harness and clip the line to a strong point.

The skipper should give you a course to steer but, if not, ask for one. If you're in sight of land he may well tell you to steer for a buoy or a tree. Even a bluffer can do that, though remember to peel off before you hit the tree. Sometimes he'll give you a compass course, for example 'Steer 220.'

There should be a compass mounted in front of the helming position, and the idea is to turn the boat until the number 220 lies beneath the line on the compass. Once there, turn the wheel a bit one way then the other and see which way the compass card moves, then turn back to 220. You'll soon get the hang of it, though nautical charts are covered in wrecks caused – presumably – by helmsman error. It's probably best not to think too much about this.

If the boat has a tiller this might take a bit more getting used to. Sit on the windward sidedeck and push the tiller away from you. The boat will turn toward the wind. Straighten up on the new course. Now pull the tiller towards you and the boat will turn back, away from the wind. Straighten up again. Repeat this until you have got the hang of the way the boat behaves.

Lovely and light on the helm

DO SAY: *I'm just seeing how responsive she is – she's lovely and light on the helm.*

DON'T SAY: *When you push the tiller to the right the boat turns left – how ridiculous! You'd think they'd have sorted that out by now.*

A bluffer should always emphasise the importance of keeping a lookout *all round* while steering. Keep standing up to scan the horizon in every direction (ensuring that one hand remains securely on the wheel or tiller). Take every opportunity to mention anything you might hit, such as other yachts, submarines, whales, large towns and so on. This will show you're doing your stuff and may prevent your being moved to a horrific job like cleaning the heads (loo).

Stopping

While steering, the bluffer will inevitably lose concentration at some stage. Rather than plough into a jetty, another boat or shallow water, it might be a good idea to slow down or even stop. Cover yourself by saying something like 'I'm assuming the skipper doesn't want me to T-bone that lovely ketch, so I'm taking no chances.' If you are beating or reaching there are two options for stopping:

Option 1. Turn slowly towards the wind. Eventually the sails will start to flap, slowing the yacht down. A further small turn and all the wind goes out of the sails and the boat stops. Now straighten up and wait for the skipper to erupt splenetically from the saloon to ask what the hell is going on.

Option 2. Keep a straight course and let out the sheets

(the ropes that control the angle of the sails to the wind). This is the second way of making the sails flap, and the boat will now slow or stop. In theory.

However, stopping on a run is trickier. Letting out the sheets won't work, because they're already eased as far as they'll go. Your only option is to anticipate the problem, giving you enough time to turn slowly *towards* the wind until the sails flap (you probably need to turn through 90 degrees or a bit more). Now straighten up and let the boat drift to a stop.

Short of taking a degree in nautical engineering you now have a good theoretical foundation on which to build a bluffing pyramid. A little knowledge may be a dangerous thing, but it does give the bluffer a head start in launching his career as the Ponzi of all things nautical. With the added bonus that you probably won't get sent to jail, unless you *really* cock things up.

Chapter 2

WHATEVER FLOATS YOUR BOAT

Once you've decided to go sailing, you'll obviously need access to a boat. This chapter aims to give you just enough knowledge to bluff yourself onto the right kind of craft or, if that fails, how to buy something suitable – only rarely advised for novice sailors (especially of the bluffing variety).

First you need to know what types of craft are available. Sailing boats are classified by *function, hull, rig* and *size*. The huge variety of boats afloat is the result of the many permutations of these characteristics. This is a posh way of saying that you can have a short fat one with one sail, a long thin one with three sails, and so on. And will Sir be using her for racing or cruising?

Function

Boats are classified by what you're going to do on them, i.e. *racing* or *cruising*. And, being realistic, there's a third (never admitted) use: *posing*.

Cruising boats need to be solidly built so they are able to survive at sea in tough conditions, can bounce off a harbour quay without collapsing and have enough living room below. Like their owners they are built more for comfort than speed, are quite broad in the beam and well upholstered.

Racing boats come in two categories:

Racing yachts have to be fast but also have to be seaworthy, with bunks so the crew can sleep between watches, galleys so someone can cook rudimentary meals at sea and have loads of space for spare sails and gear. And enough liquor to regularly splice the mainbrace. They also compete in regattas such as Cowes Week or Cork Week, where they race around buoys in the daytime then tie up together in a marina for jollification, with the sailors collapsing into their bunks at night.

Racing dinghies have only one function – winning. They have to be as light as their class rules allow, have new or nearly new sails, a polished hull and gear that works like clockwork. Be warned, an ideal dinghy crew member is expected to be an athlete, a perfectionist and feel no pain.

Posing boats seldom leave the marina. Many are little more than a waterborne gin palace, with the owner inviting people for drinks or meals 'on board my yacht.' Once on board he regales them with tales of fictitious voyages and agonises with them over the cost of ownership. Posing is, of course, akin to bluffing and both are strongly encouraged throughout this book.

Having looked at the sort of use you will make of your boat, the next step is to think about the bit that goes in the water:

The hull

Depending on your means you can choose to sail a yacht, a keelboat or a dinghy. These are mostly monohulls (one hull) but be aware that there are also catamarans (two hulls) and trimarans (three hulls).

A **yacht** has sails and a *keel*. The keel is a heavy bit of iron or lead sticking down into the water. It stops the yacht slipping sideways and levers the boat back upright when the wind tries to blow it over. A yacht also has accommodation below decks. The bluffer might like to mention that the word 'yacht' comes from the Dutch *jacht* which was originally a light and fast sailing craft used by the Dutch navy to find, pursue and capture pirates. These days yachts are used by boatbuilders to find, pursue and fleece prospective owners.

A **keelboat** also has sails and a keel. Keelboats are mainly used for shortish races so don't have accommodation (the crew will be in the bar as soon as the race finishes). Some considered keelboats a poor man's yacht, but they are probably better thought of as a rich man's dinghy.

A **dinghy** has sails but no keel. A light centreboard or daggerboard stops the boat sliding sideways but does nothing to keep the boat upright – the righting effect is provided by the crew leaning out over the side. Dinghies are cheap and fast – and fun. Though the fun bit assumes you have a six pack, don't mind swimming about after a capsize, and look good in a tight neoprene wetsuit (rather than resembling a snake that's swallowed a goat.)

Most boats only have one hull. But a catamaran is a useful alternative if you like going fast, hate heeling over (they don't) or prefer separate living (you and your spouse can sleep in separate hulls). The downside is the extra cost of duplicating things like rudders, and you'll usually pay double for mooring fees. A trimaran has a main hull in the middle with smaller hulls each side, rather like booster wheels on a kid's bike. But don't be fooled, trimarans are seriously fast. You also have to share the cabin with your spouse.

The rig

Next, a boat is defined by its *rig*, i.e. the sail(s) and mast(s). Some boats just have one mast and one sail – they are *una rigged.* A *sloop* has two sails on one mast – a jib (the small sail at the bow) and a mainsail. A *cutter* has a mainsail and two jibs. A *ketch* has two masts: the main mast rigged like a sloop and a shorter mast, the mizzen, further aft (in front of the rudder) with one sail on it. A *yawl* is similar, but the mizzen mast is right aft.

If you can remember this lot, it's Olympic standard bluffing. From your vantage point in the marina restaurant miss no opportunity to discuss the merits of the various rigs, 'That yawl has plenty of sail area but it's low down because it's spread over two masts, so she should be pretty stiff in a breeze, but probably won't point high into the wind. By comparison that sloop has a very tall mast, I bet she's really tender in a blow, though she should point well. Not sure which is better really…' With a bit of luck your bluffing skills will be sufficient to keep the argument going all the way to closing time.

Size

Size is the last piece in the jigsaw. Although a big yacht looks beautiful, it's a truism that the smaller the boat the more fun you can have. Consider a 25-footer. If you're reckless enough to buy one, you probably won't need a second mortgage; you can sail her single-handed if the crew don't turn up; you can moor in shallow water and get ashore easily. Now turn to that sleek 100-foot ketch: the owner is always in the office generating the cash to keep her afloat; he will need at least 50 occasional sailors on his Christmas card list to generate a crew of eight at any one time; and the boat's long keel will force him to anchor off in deep water, well away from the action. And, of course, if yours is the 25-footer there's nothing to stop you bluffing about her size – men have been doing that for centuries. By the time your potential crew actually see your little craft it'll be too late for them to back out.

OK, now you have an idea of what's available, think for a minute what sort of boat will suit you best. Then decide how you're going to get on board such a craft.

Hitching a ride

Naturally, the best way to go sailing is on someone else's boat. Let the owner worry about the initial cost, depreciation, upkeep and mooring fees. And never forget that you are actually in a strong position: he can't go sailing without a crew and from his position on Fantasy Island (i.e. the cockpit) he is helpless unless the crew decide to humour him by casting off, pulling up the sails, tacking and so on. Initially you will have to bluff that you like taking orders, love getting wet on the foredeck, enjoy cooking with the boat on its ear and don't snore. But once afloat you can relax and revert to the crew's normal attitude of insolent laziness, since the owner is stuck with you for the rest of the weekend.

However, if you overplay this advice or failed to bluff properly in the first place, you may find yourself short of a ride. In this catastrophic situation you may even be forced to contemplate buying your own boat. In a feeble last attempt to put you off this disastrous course of action the rest of this chapter outlines all the problems of the purchase and, of course, explains how to get rid of the damn thing when you finally realise your mistake.

Buying your own

To mitigate the size of your impending disaster, look first for a second-hand boat. A good tactic is to put yourself in the mindset of the seller – he will inevitably be fed up with the boat, with sailing or even with life itself. So, if you want to buy a racing dinghy a good place to start is at the end of the National Championship, where disgruntled owners naturally blame the boat for their lack of success. If you strike at this moment of maximum gloom you can pick up a good bargain. Similarly, if you want to buy a seagoing yacht, the Spanish city of La Coruna is a good place to begin. This is the first port of call after crossing the Bay of Biscay, one of the roughest bits of sea in the world. After pitching about green-gilled for two or three days without sleep, many owners' first thought on landing is to get as far away from the sea as possible and their yachts sprout 'For Sale' signs quicker than you can say 'Bargain'.

If this tactic fails you will have to fall back on the ads in the back of sailing magazines, trawl the internet or go to a broker and read the details of the boats on his books. In every case the purple prose makes Estate Agents' particulars look positively truthful: this is professional bluffing. Deceptively spacious the boat may be, but if the keel bolts are half rusted away or the mast is about to fall down you won't find *that* in the blurb.

Thus, in the spirit of helping fellow sufferers, we offer below some examples to help reading between the lines of these classified adverts.

YACHTS FOR SALE

Advert Says	The Truth
Ideal project for the DIY enthusiast	Boat completely knackered
In every sense a family boat	Really slow. Chintzy décor
Sleeps six	Four bunks. The rest sleep on the floor
Full of character	Lots of stupid modifications
Has had very little use	A bugger to sail
Carefully maintained	Needs loads of work each winter
Cruiser/racer	Uncomfortable for cruising, slow for racing
Highly competitive	We tried everything but never won a race
Lively performance	Bounces around dreadfully at sea
Ideal fishing boat	Hopeless under sail
Motor sailer	Sails like a snail, needs the engine at all times
Ideal first boat	You'll want to sell it at the end of the season
Many extras	Opportunity to clear the garage of all the boat's tat
Needs some work	Needs everything replacing
Includes six months' mooring	Half a season was more than enough
Rare opportunity to purchase	All her sister ships have sunk
Reluctantly for sale	Spouse insists we sell it
No reasonable offer refused	Owner desperate
For immediate sale	Owner about to go down for ten years

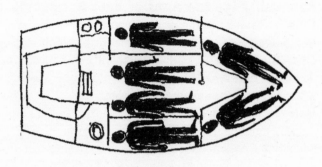

For sale: Yacht Armistad – sleeps six

DINGHIES FOR SALE

Advert Says	The Truth
Ready to win	Hasn't won yet
Good racing record	Lots of 4ths and 5ths but no podium finish
Winning boat	Won the 1976 Ladies' Race
Many extras	Tons of stuff you don't need
Well maintained	A pain to paint and varnish every winter
Owner changing class	All the other boats in this class are faster
One season's use	A windy season knocked the stuffing out of everything

Armed with this info you can weed out the non-starters and draw up a shortlist of boats to view.

Remember the ten rules of boat purchasing

Rule 1. Check out the owner on the web. You may find him bragging on social media to his friends about a dodgy channel crossing – perhaps involving hitting a rock, damaging the keel and bending the rudder post. Useful info when you're discussing the price later.

Rule 2. Ask third parties about the boat, e.g. the harbour master, neighbouring skippers, earlier owners. 'She was lying on the bottom until they raised her a couple of months ago. You'll still find seaweed in the lockers.'

Rule 3. Find someone with a similar boat and ask them what to look for, e.g. 'The roller reefing never works on a Tolpuddle 325. It costs a fortune to sort that out.'

Rule 4. Be early. Then you can carry out Step 2 in person, and may even see the owner bailing out, filling cracks, and so on.

Rule 5. Turkish carpet salesmen are expert at putting you under an obligation, e.g. by giving you tea and baklava. So don't accept food or drink or a lift from the vendor.

Rule 6. Try not to fall in love with the boat. Make a costed list of all the things that need fixing – that should cool your ardour.

Rule 7. Pre-set your budget and tell someone else the amount. Then you can't creep upwards if Rule 6 fails.

Rule 8. Insist on a test sail. Don't be fooled by the owner bluffing that he has to be back in the office by 4pm: set all the sails and run the engine, the fridge, the cooker and all the electronics.

Rule 9. Ask why they're selling. 'Getting a larger boat' is understandable. 'Giving up sailing' is suspicious.

Rule 10. Don't fall for bluffing or flattery. 'This does look just your sort of boat; I could see the moment you took the helm that you know what you're doing. She'll look after you on long ocean passages and has a good turn of speed on the racecourse.' Strange, since your only sailing has been in an old Enterprise on a gravel pit.

A new boat

All this test sailing can become tedious, and in the end you may decide to up the ante and go for a new boat. You then have three options: buy her off-the-shelf, build her yourself, or commission a yard to build one. A bluffer is strongly advised to do none of the above. To a boatbuilder 'BOAT' stands for 'Bung On Another Thousand'.

Selling a boat

As the saying goes: If buying a boat is the happiest day of your life, the second happiest is the day you sell it.

Having been through all the seller's bluffing when you bought your craft, the seaboot is now on the other trotter. Devise an irresistible advert, agree to a viewing only on a day when the sun is shining and the wind is Force 4. Collect your potential victims from the station and ply them with lunch and alcohol in the sparkling saloon of your so-reasonably-priced yacht. Borrow the expert crew from your club's fastest yacht and take everyone out for a sail. Do some racing tacks and gybes, followed by lots of nifty spinnaker work. Congratulate the prospective purchaser on his helming and leadership, and his partner on their youthfulness, crewing skills and sporting enthusiasm for their project (in that order). Then head ashore with *Another One Bites the Dust* on the cockpit speakers. Who could resist? The boat's as good as sold.

This chapter has been about what might be called The Standard Sailing Cycle:

1. Buy boat
2. Sail it
3. Sell it
4. Lament the loss of £100k
5. Treasure the wonderful memories

Now it's time to dress for the part.

Chapter 3

GET THE LOOK

Although you may not have any sailing skills at all, looking the part is a key element in the armoury of a bluffer. It's one of the few occasions when throwing money at the problem may actually work.

In fact, you will need to splash quite a bit of cash because you'll need different outfits for yachting (in both foul and fair weather), dinghy sailing and, most importantly, going on a run ashore. With luck this chapter might just prevent your being scoffed at by the rest of the crew.

Yachting in bad weather

When the going gets tough the bluffer gets going – preferably below, where it's warm, dry and he can perfect his outfit.

Air is a good insulator. Considering that it's free, it's ironic that expensive clothing contains a lot of it. Air is also the key reason for putting on *layers* of clothing in the hope that the air between them will keep you warm. This also gives bluffing opportunities for you to discuss your kit as you put it on: 'I always go for a technical performance base layer to minimise loss of body heat, then a quick-dry mid-layer for further temperature regulation. Alternatively, if the

29

conditions aren't too severe I sometimes go for wool, which seems to keep sheep happy, or a fleece one-piece (I call it a babygrow)...' This drivel shows you mean business but is boring enough to get you some peace while you wrestle with the intricacies of your new gear.

Next you'll need thermal socks, and shoes. If your audience is still awake you can comment that you've found deck shoes are useless in the wet because they take ages to dry so, after trying everything, your preference is Gore-Tex boots. If you are in fact planning to wear your gardening wellies explain that, sadly, you left your Dubarrys on the Commodore's yacht so are reduced to your Hunters.

Over all this lot you will need oilskins. Perhaps not the sexiest of garments, but the ones that define your place in the sartorial pecking order, since a jacket and trousers can cost anything between £50 and £1,500. Yes, really. If you want to be stunningly flash choose a set with strips of reflecting material so you look really hip at night (a secondary benefit is that people can see you by torchlight when you fall in). And, however much you paid, buff up your suit with plenty of dirt and grease before you use it, otherwise you'll be rumbled as a newbie.

Another option is to buy some oilies second-hand at a boat jumble, and the inevitable grime will give the authentic look. They'll also give you the chance to mention that: 'they previously belonged to Chay Blyth and have been round the world twice... they still had a Mars bar in the pocket when I bought them, it's amazing that they're still waterproof, but I guess that quality will out. I reckon Chay probably regrets selling them.'

Still had a Mars bar in the pocket

Finally the hard bit – putting on your lifejacket and harness. (Remember to put them on OVER your oilies or you may be suffocated when the lifejacket inflates or, worse, bursts the stitching on your expensive jacket.) The hard bit is that all the webbing straps look the same and you want your arms through the arm loops and your legs through the crutch straps. If you get them the other way round you could cover your embarrassment by standing on your head, which might get a laugh and even an offer of help. In fact getting this lot right is really a two-man job and even then you may both finish up in the same lifejacket.

Lastly, check where the inflating toggle is situated, as you may need to pull it in an emergency. It's important to keep the toggle under control or it may catch as you come out of the companionway and inflate the lifejacket, trapping you in the hatchway like an obese Santa in a chimney. (Claiming that the mechanism is faulty might be worth a tentative bluff at this point, but a cynical crew will probably be laughing too loudly to hear you.)

DO SAY: *Super oilies, Jason.*
DON'T SAY: *You look as though you've been poured into those waterproofs and forgotten to say "When".*

So now, after a mere half an hour, you are dressed for action. After all the exertion you're probably feeling a bit queasy, but if you can hold on it might be worth taking a moment to accessorise your ensemble. Start at the top and work down:
• Put on a peaked cap *under* the hood of your oilies. Not over it. Then when you turn your head, the hood will turn

with you, as opposed to your face disappearing into the static hood. The peak also keeps the rain / spray out of your eyes.

- Shades are always cool. Never forget the famous Jack Nicholson quote: 'With my sunglasses on I'm Jack Nicholson. Without them I'm fat and 60.'

- A hefty horizontal stripe of white sunblock from cheek to cheek across your nose looks really macho. Ignore any sniggering references to Adam Ant.

- A scarf stops drips going down your neck. Using a tea towel from the galley demonstrates a measure of nonchalance.

- Have a cork float on your keyring. Pulling it out of your pocket will give you the chance to mention the time you lost all your keys overboard in mid-Pacific, 'Sadly it was above the Mariana Trench which, as you'll know, is 11,000 metres deep. After that I always make sure they float...'

- A flashy sailing watch allows you to pontificate about the state of the tide, the weather forecast, your latitude and longitude, and when your next haircut is due. But don't wear it when the clocks change – the algorithm is more complex than the Space-Time Continuum and you'll be revealed as a bluffer if you can't move the hour forward or back.

- Sporting a music player with earphones completes your gear. It not only shows you know how to keep awake on long night watches, it's also handy to drown out the skipper's expletives when you screw up on the foredeck.

Yachting in fine weather

Really, when the sun shines anything goes. A captain's hat, braid, cravat, white flannels and two-tone brogues are best kept in the fancy dress box. You will probably sport deck shoes, shorts, cap, shades and a T-shirt.

A run ashore

For a bluffer, the best thing about sailing is when it stops. That ends the struggle to prove your competence, and you can finally re-enter your natural habitat on *terra firma*.

The pub or restaurant may beckon but do take a moment to at least change your jeans. A shower will also help, particularly if you have people of another gender on board. Male sailors are always amazed that females can enter the heads damp, wind-swept and crusted in salt and emerge a few minutes later fragrant, fully made up, hair in place and in a strappy LBD ready for a sophisticated soiree.

> **DO SAY:** *Samantha, that dress looks fantastic.*
> **DON'T REPLY:** *Oh, it's just some old thing I threw on.*
> **THEN DEFINITELY DON'T SAY:** *Wow! And you nearly missed.*

Bear in mind that many shoreside expeditions begin with a row ashore in the dinghy. This guarantees you will arrive with a wet bottom so consider wearing your oilskin trousers. Sometimes you will need to wade ashore so wear your wellies and carry your brothel creepers to put on later. In fact the logical conclusion you may come to is to carry a complete set of dry clothing in a waterproof bag – this way

Don't get turned away

you won't get turned away when you arrive at the swanky eatery oozing mud and seaweed.

A final tip – remember where the yacht is. If the evening goes well, you'll be coming back to the boat after dark. In the gloaming, after a few pints, one yacht looks much like another at anchor and it's no fun rowing about the bay trying to find yours. Hanging a distinctive light in the rigging overcomes this problem and shows what an experienced sailor you are. This principle holds good even if the boat is in a marina, where there may be hundreds of similar yachts. Hoisting a skull and crossbones should do the trick.

Dressing for dinghy sailing

In a dinghy you're close to the water and will usually get wet, which tends to make you cold. Most people solve this problem by wearing a wetsuit or, in the winter, a drysuit.

A *wetsuit* is made of rubber and traps water between it and your skin. Your body warms this water and the effect is like wearing a tepid hot water bottle. A further plus is that the wetsuit also pads you from getting knocked by the boat's sharp edges and dulls the pain when you sit out (hike) over the side of the boat to keep it upright.

This padding can be enhanced by putting battens in slots in the legs of the wetsuit, enabling you to hike even further out without cutting off the supply of blood to your legs. Don't miss the opportunity to bluff that you keep a hiking bench in front of the telly so you can train: 'I find it surprising that I can only manage ten minutes at a time on the bench, whereas in a race I have no problem hiking hard for two hours or more...' (In fact two minutes on a bench would nearly kill you, as would ten minutes hiking on the dinghy.)

Unless you're sailing a trapeze boat, you will continually be scootching your glutes fore-and-aft and in-and-out on the deck to trim the boat, and in no time will have a hole in your wetsuit with your backside hanging out of it. It may be your best feature but for once it's best covered up: the cool thing is to wear a natty pair of sacrificial shorts over the wetsuit, and when they're nearly worn through patch them with a beer towel from your local bar. Your helmsman might take the hint and buy you a pint of the brew your bottom is promoting.

As with cruising, a lifejacket or buoyancy aid goes over your wetsuit. This should have a pocket for some spare split-rings and a shackle or two. A cap, shades, wetboots and leather gloves complete the ensemble.

A *drysuit* is a bit like the suit worn by an old-fashioned diver (without the helmet). It's made of waterproof material with rubber seals at neck and wrist, and rubber socks bonded to the legs. Unlike a wetsuit its objective is to keep you dry, and the warmth comes from what you're wearing underneath. Ignore the way James Bond peeled off his drysuit to reveal a dinner jacket and buttonhole, your style is more to sport a fluffy babygrow. You may not dazzle a beautiful Russian spy, but you'll come ashore dry and warm.

As with all good things, a drysuit comes with a catch – getting out of it is a nightmare. Practise at home because the club changing room is no place to be trapped inside it.

There is in fact only one way to free yourself:

1. Undo the zip.

2. Using your right hand, pull down on the left cuff and

keep pulling.
3. Ease your left elbow up the sleeve until your left arm is out of the sleeve and in the suit.
4. Pull the rubber neck seal over your head.
5. Ease your body out through the zip.
6. Peel down the suit over your legs.

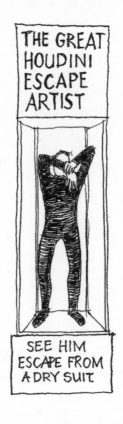

Easy really, especially after a couple of days of practising. Once you can do this, the drysuit becomes your friend again. And removing it quickly and *slickly* gives you the opportunity to bluff about your previous career as a professional diver.

Carrying it off

Now you've got The Look you can use further props to reveal your sailing expertise.

Emerge from your bunk in your boxers and vest, your stubble unshaved. You are the epitome of nautical *toughness*. 'Luckily, I don't feel the cold. That's why I always jump at the chance to sail in high latitudes, though I must admit we were once caught in the ice in the Bering Strait. That was a bit chilly.'

Put on your T-shirt with a cheeky logo, e.g. *Luff 'em and leave 'em* or *Winch wenches do it in turns*. This shows you have a nautical *sense of humour*.

Don a Breton sweater, ghastly red trousers and a sou'wester to mark you out as a nautical *traditionalist*. 'Standards are slipping horribly. That yacht is flying a blue ensign at the stern but no burgee at the masthead. No doubt the Queen will be revoking his warrant...'

An ostentatious opening of your multitool, revealing screwdrivers, a mini magnifying glass, etc. marks you down as someone *practical*. 'I always have a spare length of rope in my pocket. When the tiller extension broke in the Nationals last year, I was able to tie my bit of string round the tiller and steer her to windward from the sidedeck.'

You get the idea. With all the gear and, now, a seafaring persona, let your imagination fly.

Chapter 4

SHIPMATES AHOY!

Even more important than choosing a boat and your gear is finding good people to sail with. Indeed, one of the Royal sailing clubs has an overarching criterion when choosing new members: could you see yourself spending a wet weekend on a small yacht with this person?

If finding the right shipmates is that important, you might benefit from some guidance here. Otherwise you could well find yourself setting sail with a crew handpicked from the cast of *Pirates of the Caribbean* (no make-up required).

Optimists & pessimists

A pessimist is someone who climbs to the top of a tall mast, falls off and on the way down shouts 'I'm going to die.' He hits the deck and does indeed peg out.

An optimist falls off the same mast. Halfway down he yells 'So far so good.' As he passes the boom he quips 'I may be a bit late for lunch.'

In fact you probably need both types on a boat. Choose to sail with a pessimistic navigator because he'll always be looking ahead to see what can go wrong. That's pretty handy when there are rocks about. But choose an optimistic owner because he may honestly believe that sailing is well within his means. And *that's* pretty handy when you crash his yacht into a jetty, rip the spinnaker or catch the mast on an overhead cable.

(Note: if you plan to do all three at once it might be helpful to lighten the mood with a bluff along the lines of: 'When I last caught a mast on an electric cable the insurance company were happy to cough up £30k for a new rig. This seemed generous until they mentioned that it was a drop in the ocean – we had blacked out Southampton for two hours and *that* bill was £2 million. So all-in-all, Skip, it puts our little accident into perspective…')

Top brass

Sailing does seem to attract its share of brigadiers, wing commanders and admirals. These guys are great at managing a large group of men who will obey orders from on high come what may, but it doesn't always work that well on a small boat. Indeed, it's often said that the most useless things on a yacht are a wheelbarrow, an umbrella and a naval officer.

Where the military do come in handy is doing things they've been trained to do: keeping the radio working, the engine running, wading through mud to lay out the anchor, doing without sleep and, of course, finding licensed premises. That's presumably why the army places such emphasis on reading maps, and it certainly pays off when you're thirsty in a strange port. Plus, once in the bar, the military are brilliant at chatting up the locals, even ones of the same sex.

The sailing bore

There's nothing worse than sailing with someone who can only talk about sailing. That's your job. But there you are, in a nice restaurant and up he pipes. 'Last week you won't believe what happened at the windward mark. Look, the salt can be the buoy, I'm this fork and the spoon is this other boat. I came into the buoy on starboard, the other boat came in on port and tacked under my bow. There was another boat coming back downwind like this knife...' And on and on.

The guy doesn't realise that any decent sailor should have at least three interests. When you're doing one of them the unwritten rule is that you only talk about the other two. For example, when you're sailing you should only talk about golf and sex. When you're golfing talk about sailing and sex, and when you're having sex talk about golf and sailing.

Talk about sailing during sex

On second thoughts, maybe this isn't the best example, but you get the idea. If you fail to persuade the bore to change tack you may need to take drastic action. How about a version of the famous solution invented by the author Saki: as you leave the restaurant together push ahead through the door, loudly commenting 'I believe I take precedence: you are merely the ship's bore but I am the ship's bluffer.' That should shut him up for a bit.

Foreigners

Of course your shipmates may not all be English or even, for heaven's sake, British. So it would be remiss not to mention some national characteristics that you may encounter on board.

American sailors tend to talk big and make things complex. For example, we tend to think a sail should last 'at least a couple of seasons.' An American will advise 'after six races any sail is absolutely shot.' We might ask for the spinnaker pole to be pulled in until it's square to the wind, then pulled in a tad more. The American will call for it to be 'over trimmed by 17 degrees.' And apparently they believe that if you pull in a sheet in a Californian accent 'it's worth half a knot.' No wonder the special relationship is in trouble.

Italian sailors believe all rules are there to be broken. In the same way that an Italian driver will go through a red light because 'they're just advisory', they expect to get away with crossing the start line early, pumping the sails in and out, running the engine when no-one's listening and turning round before they reach the buoy. (Actually, now you mention it, some of these might be worth a try.)

French sailors are used to the sunshine and like to sail naked. This can be something of a problem for the Brits on board, who are used to having a spare sail tie in their pocket and rely on clamping a flogging genoa (see Glossary) between their knees so they have both hands free to lower the sail. And in any case, where do those Frenchies keep their mobiles?

Australian sailors are surprisingly polite and humorous. Do mention the time you pulled in the jib a bit fast and fell backwards onto the lap of an Aussie crewman. Far from a string of expletives, all he said was 'Strewth mate, we haven't even been introduced.' This is not only funny but pokes fun at the British, a prime Australian pastime.

The **Swedes** are fantastic sailors, especially considering that their season only runs from July till September. (Outside of that the boats are cocooned ashore, to protect them from the long icy winter.) Most people sail on bits of water with a few rocks, but the Swedes have rocks everywhere with bits of water in between. This makes them wonderful navigators – thus enabling their Vikings to clamp on their horned helmets and sail abroad, pillaging at will.

Sailing for seniors

The other point to make about your fellow crewmates is that you can expect them to be any age, since sailing is one of the few sports that you can literally do from birth till death. As a cultural bluff you could mention that even Shakespeare, living miles from the sea in Stratford, got this right in his *Seven Ages of Man* speech:

'At first the infant, mewling and puking' pretty well sums

up life at sea for a baby, and 'sans teeth, sans eyes, sans taste, sans everything' pretty well sums up the geriatric sailor – broke, obviously, but also deaf:

SKIPPER: *Abandon ship!*
GERIATRIC: *Yes, lovely trip!*

and blind:

GERIATRIC: *The fog's getting thicker, I can't see a thing.*
SKIPPER: *Actually, you're sitting inside the sprayhood.*

Finding a role on a yacht

After reading this lot you should be sufficiently sea-wise to have selected good crewmates. Now you have to turn to the various positions on a yacht, so that when you get on board you can choose a job that best suits your nautical skill set. (If you don't have a skill set, this section should at least let you bluff yourself through for a couple of days.) Start at the bow and work aft through Fantasy Island to the stern. We assume you're on a racing yacht with a big crew; but the same jobs have to be done with a smaller crew on a cruising boat, so there you may be expected to combine several roles.

The Bowman

This is a slot that no one wants, because it's cold and wet and well away from the warmth of the saloon. There's not much conversation either, since the rest of the crew are snuggled down well aft in the cockpit. On the plus side the bowman is too far forward to hear the expletives from the crew boss and is really in control of any manoeuvre: if he decides to put up the No 2 genoa, get the kedge anchor ready or clip on the small spinnaker there's not really much anyone else can do about it.

If you want to be a successful bowman you need to bulk up – those sails are heavy as is the spinnaker pole when it's dropped on your head. You'll need bigger clothes, of course – any self-respecting bowman looks like an escaped marquee.

The Grinder

The ropes (sheets and control lines) are led back to the cockpit. Hauling them in is the job of the grinder; his idea of a good time is winding in the genoa sheet fast during a series of short tacks. Other co-workers should keep well out of the way because, if you're touching the sheet, it's easy to get your fingers wound into the winch – and hard to make the gorilla with the winch handle stop winding.

But most of the time there is no winding to do, and the grinder just sits on the rail and helps keep the boat upright. Thus grinders need to be heavy as well as muscle-bound. They tend to have nicknames like Shorty or Tiny and consume huge chunks of the ship's stores at each meal. If you fancy this position you can practise at home by (a) pulling the lawnmower's starter cord 1,000 times and (b) sitting still and meditating. If this doesn't put you off, you may have found your niche.

The Trimmer

Once the grinder has used brute force to wind in the sheets

and has muscled in the other control lines, the stage is set for the trimmer to fine tune the settings for sail shape and speed. On a racing yacht everything is adjusted constantly, on most cruising boats you just cleat the ropes and put on the kettle.

A good trimmer has a real eye for sail shape and can really make a difference by pulling in the outhaul an inch or loosening off the kicker a tad. This is ideal territory for the bluffer – just keep your control line going in and out about its original setting, all the while commenting 'Pressure coming, down on the traveller, backstay on please, I'm tightening the Cunningham (see Glossary)...'

If you're too lazy to wind in your rope the grinder will pull it in for you – surely even you won't find letting it *out* too onerous. But do remember to always put several turns of the rope round a winch first – there can be a huge force involved and if you just release the cleat the rope will fly out burning your hands. Since you chose trimming to avoid hard work and preserve your manicure, this may not please you.

Always put several turns around the winch

The Navigator

> **QUESTION**: *Why are so many pubs called* The Hope and Anchor*?*
> **ANSWER**: *Because, in days of old, when the navigator had screwed up bigtime and the boat was heading for the rocks, the last resort was to pull the sails down, drop the anchor and hope it held the boat off the lee shore until the wind dropped.*

Sadly this often didn't work, but it does make the point that navigation is pretty important.

Actually navigation is about two things: *Where are we?* and *Where are we going?* The ancient sailor only ever had a rough idea where he was, which caused most of his problems. Plus his charts were inaccurate or non-existent, so he couldn't plot a reliable course to his destination. If *you* fancy being a navigator you've got it easy: the GPS tells you to within a few metres where you are, and the electronic (and paper) charts show your destination and the hazards along the way. All you have to do is set up the system, then an arrow on the screen shows the boat's progress along the desired route.

Have a dummy run at home to see if this job appeals. Find a teenager and get them to download some electronic charts onto your tablet, and a program to run them. Then imagine a voyage and put in waypoints on the chart to take you to your target skirting shallows, rocks and so forth. Finally get the wunderkind to give you enough tech terms for realistic bluffing later. (There is, of course, nothing to stop you planning a real trip in this way at home, and you'll get a lot of brownie points if you come on board with this groundwork done.)

For bluffing at sea you'll have to speak in acronyms, so you might as well mug up on those too. Then plan some simple sentences so you'll look good: 'How's the SOG going skip?' 'What's our COG?' 'The BTW should be 325 True.' 'I hope the CTE isn't building!' Honestly, real navigators do talk like this.

And if you really want to know, here's the translation:

- **SOG** = Speed Over the Ground
- **COG** = Course Over the Ground
- **BTW** = Bearing to Waypoint
- **CTE** = Cross Track Error

The Tactician

The navigator works down below and the helmsman is, of course, on deck. The tactician moves between them. His job is to work out the best route from one buoy or waypoint to the next, and to steer the craftiest course to defeat the opposition. He spends most of his time watching the compass for windshifts and whispering instructions into the helmsman's ear.

A tactician is there to talk, so you'll have to bluff more than in most positions. Here are some good phrases to use, even if your motive is suspect:

The Sailor's Bluffing Bible

What You Say	What You Really Mean
The starboard end of the line is best	There are fewer boats there and less to worry about
We're being headed, let's tack	I'm getting cold, we'll be in the sun on the other tack
Carry on, we're crossing them	I hope to goodness we're ahead
Slam tack!	Oops! We weren't
Trim the genoa sheet please	Why are we going like a dog?
What's the bearing to the mark?	I've no idea where we are
Tack to cover the red boat	Forget the rest of the fleet. That's the guy who owes me £20
It's fastest to finish at the port end	I need a beer and that end's nearest to the marina

If you can keep up this rubbish for the whole race, you may have a great tactical future on the boat.

The Helmsman

This is the easiest job on the boat. All you have to do is look as though you're concentrating and occasionally move your hand six inches or so.

Tacking is really fun: you shout 'Ready about' and put the wheel over, then all hell breaks loose. Crew scurry across the cabin top to the other side, the trimmers cast off the old sheets, the sails flog and the grinders wind like crazy to get the new sheets in. At the end all you do is straighten up and mention that they could have been a little quicker.

Easiest job on the boat

A gybe is even more fun. Once again your job is to shout 'Gybe ho' then simply to turn the boat a bit. Everyone else has to rupture themselves getting the boom over, pulling the genoa across the deck, gybing the spinnaker, grabbing the bowman as the spinnaker pole knocks him overboard and so on. From your position on the wheel, you have a perfect view of the whole circus.

If you are the sort of person who likes to be the centre of attention but doesn't like to do much work (i.e. a quintessential bluffer) then this is the job for you. Oh, and make sure you don't hit anything while you're busy watching the crew's antics, or your job may be a short one.

What to do on a dinghy

With all these possible bluffing positions on a yacht, I'm afraid you'll find yourself short-changed on a dinghy. Sailing a single-handed dinghy leaves you no-one to bluff to, so that's not an option.

A double-hander isn't much better because the helmsman is usually the owner (and you've been warned against going down that route) and the crew is just there to be shouted at by the helmsman. You won't get a word in edgeways, let alone be able to bluff.

So, when dinghy sailing, you will be restricted to bluffing ashore in the sailing club, which we turn to next. If, that is, you can find a club lax enough to let you bluff yourself in.

Chapter 5

JOIN THE CLUB

If you want to see a gathering of bluffers, look no further than your local sailing club. There, safely on dry land, nobody can tell if the raconteur can really sail, forecast the weather or navigate. (Although one aspiring bluffer who professed to be a navigator was famously unable to find his way *to the bar*, which was a bit of a give-away.)

For the bluffer there's a huge range of clubs to choose from. Usually the name reveals all, thus Mudpuddle Sailing Club is probably on a small gravel pit and the level of sailing should be comfortingly low. On arrival, make clear that your normal sailing ground is rather more grand: 'I'm looking forward to sailing here. Super to be independent of the tide, I've fallen foul of the Portland Race so many times...'

The Birmingham Cruising Club could also be an option, Brum being about as far from the sea as you can get in the UK. Even if you do get dragged along to their annual cruise, you're unlikely to sail far – maybe from Southampton to Cowes, and even a bluffer can avoid being sick for that long.

On arrival there will be merry banter about how they got there – methods like GPS, Dead Reckoning, taking fixes and using a sextant will be claimed. Now is your chance to shine – advanced bluffing would be: 'I found it difficult to shoot the sun at noon, but taken alongside a running fix and the GPS we were pretty well spot-on when we arrived in Cowes.' (Don't get too carried away though, you can almost *see* Cowes from Southampton.)

Beware any club with Royal in its title, as this is an indication that things may be taken a bit more seriously. You will probably have to wear a tie and blazer (they call it a reefer) in the clubhouse and fly a blue ensign at the back of the boat (the stern). This is a pain because you are required to get out of your bunk early in the morning to fly it and have to remember to lower it at 8pm (or dusk) in the evening. You also have to fly a little flag (a burgee) at the top of the mast, where it normally gets tangled up in the radio aerial, thus preventing calls for help or phoning your mother for cooking advice. If you *must* take your G and T at the Royal Yacht Squadron (known just as 'The Squadron') be ready to up your bluffing a notch, e.g. 'Are 'The Family' attending Cowes Week this year? Poor things, it can't be the same for them without Britannia.' (Pronounced 'Bwitannyah'.)

The interview

The first step to joining your chosen club may be an interview with a member of The Committee, such as the Vice Commodore. Try to avoid asking how much vice he is planning for the season – rather than gloomily suffering quips he has heard a thousand times before, he'll be looking for things you can do for the club. Drinking heavily at the bar is, surprisingly, a plus here because it's good for the club's finances. Sneak into the bar before the interview and see what they are flogging, then you can mention that you are looking forward to extensive sampling of the club's excellent Taylor Fladgate '55 / Merlot / London Pride / Fanta (or whatever).

Keenness to do your 'duties' is a winner: you will probably have to do two anyway so you may as well pretend to like them. Don't let yourself in for anything technical, rather say something like: 'I'd normally offer to be Officer of the Day, I used to run the Championships at the Royal Corgi YC, but as things are now... (*pause... sigh... sad distant gaze...*) I guess I could do the teas or some hack work.'

And don't forget to mention the other clubs you've belonged to.

The Imperial Poona is a good one because they only have 25 members (which did include Prince Philip) and no one knows that the objectives of the club are to 'think imperially' and sail the course backwards. (Yes, really.) They do this wearing a pith helmet over a red and yellow tie, by the way.

Staying a member

After that lot, you should be voted in. Now all you've got to do is avoid being chucked out again by falling foul of one of the club's characters or making an error of etiquette.

Beware the Club Hottie. They are the only one allowed in the clubhouse in micro shorts and a skimpy top. A new member typically begins chatting them up before realising that they're the Vice Commodore's spouse or, worse, engaged to the Handicap Secretary (you'll never win with a poor handicap). If you're caught ogling, try something like 'I was admiring the slogan on your T-shirt. I think my partner would fancy one like that. *'Happiness is a smooth bottom'* is so profound.'

Beware the Club Hottie

Equally lethal is the club bore. If you let him buy you a drink, you'll never get rid of him. So use a blocking bluff like 'Thanks, but it was too dangerous to drink on the Atlantic crossings and somehow I've never gone back to alcohol.'

If he counters by buying you a fizzy water begin a long diatribe on water conservation aboard: 'The skipper made me stand in the shower naked, fully soaped-up, clutching a ready-pasted toothbrush and with my laundry under my feet. Only then would he turn on the water. You clean your teeth, trample your smalls and wash your body at the same time and should easily finish before he turns the water off after 90 seconds. But, of course, a water-maker would have changed the whole game...' After half an hour of this drivel he should leave you alone. There's only room for one bore in a conversation.

Finally, beware the skipper recruiting crew. Alarm bells should ring if he:

1. Asks you to come sailing (he's never met you before, and anyway is clearly a bad judge of character).
2. Has no other crew for the trip.
3. Says the boat is forty years old but has 'never had a problem'.

The lack of crew may indicate a man who shouts a lot, never says please, doesn't do chores or cook, snores, is mean, farts continually... and those are some of his better qualities.

A forty-year-old boat that hasn't been maintained is lethal. A yacht is a delicate instrument surrounded by corrosive liquid and crewed by cack-handed incompetents. Something will break or need fixing *every day*.

If he is pushing you to go and you suspect the trip is doomed, then you'll need escape bluffing. Try one of the following:

- 'Great idea, provided I can bring my friend. We can stow his wheelchair in the stern locker and his guide dog's toilet training is coming on...'
- 'My dad was on a boat once and the keel fell off. I assume you don't mind my withdrawing a keel bolt to check for corrosion? Of course you'll have to crane her out to do

that – £750 should cover it.'
- 'Insurance companies demand that the rigging is replaced every 10 years. I imagine you've done that – if not we can do it at the same time as the keel.'
- 'Super invite, thanks! As soon as my left hip has been replaced, I'm your man.'

(Further cast-iron excuses when declining an invitation to crew can be found in the following chapter).

Welcome on board

If, despite all the advice given here, you do take up an invitation to go sailing, you might as well ingratiate yourself from the start. Miracles do happen, and you might actually *want* to be asked back!

The drink on most boats is pretty awful, having been sloshed about in the bilge for months or sometimes even years. Please the skipper by donating some whisky, creating a bluffing opportunity to describe your booze cruise up the west coast of Scotland: 'Wonderful week, sailing from distillery to distillery. Amazing how I could navigate completely legless.' Alternatively, take some French plonk in plastic bottles: 'Just something we brought back from the race to Le Havre. Had to be plastic I'm afraid, it was a bit bumpy – six metre waves all the way back.'

Most yachts have a bewildering number of ropes on deck, led back to a row of cleats on the cabin top. If you take a roll of tape and a magic marker you can then ask the skipper to label each cleat – 'Main halyard', 'Vang' and so on. This gives you the opportunity to mention that you 'always do this on racing yachts.' It will, of course, help you pull the right rope when he yells 'Pull the vang!' 'Let off the halyard!' and other gibberish. (It's also a good idea to go below in a quiet moment and look up on your mobile what a vang actually *does*, what a main halyard *is*, and so on.) This tip is a prime example of a bluffer thinking ahead (for once).

Finally, as you have been advised more than once in this erudite volume, take with you the weather forecast and the time of high tide. At the beginning of the trip everyone will have an opinion about where and when to sail, but not all will have done this relatively basic homework. Feign surprise, saying it's second nature to you.

Chapter 6

I'D LOVE TO, BUT...

Must I go down to the sea again?

Let's face it, it's cold and wet out there. Except for the one day a year when the sun's out and the wind's Force 4, a bluffer is better off in the bar.

Declining an invitation to crew

Despite the best endeavours of a bluffer, skippers are desperate for crew. Over the years they have become adept at presenting themselves and their craft as world leaders in hospitality and luxury. After a few beers you may be lured into this web and, a few days later, find yourself greeted by a portly little sociopath in ill-fitting shorts and a Hawaiian shirt standing by the most unseaworthy of boats.

It was to avoid just this sort of calamity that this book was written. Here are four tried and tested excuses for saying 'no' to sailing invitations, followed by a manual for survival if you were too drunk to remember them and said 'yes'.

1. PTSD (Post Traumatic Sailing Disorder)

This is an excellent bluff because it gives you the opportunity to dwell on your heroic actions in extreme conditions.

DO SAY: *After the '79 Fastnet I swore I'd never go to sea again. Twelve hours before the storm and twelve hours afterwards we were becalmed but when the storm hit we were in shallow waters off The Rock and the seas really got a bit lumpy. We heard reports of other yachts turning turtle and people taking to their liferafts. I managed to keep up morale by singing a selection of classic sea shanties while steering through the breakers and plotting a course for Plymouth. Needless to say I have sailed again but never in*

winds above Force 4 or in boats of less than 60 feet.
DON'T SAY: *I tried sailing once but my hat blew off, followed shortly by my favourite toupee. Never again!*

Love to join you but the idiot skipper crash-gybed; I tried to save the boom but...

2. The Old War Wound Is Playing Up

Actually you may not get away with this. But claiming to have damaged yourself during nautical action is a legitimate excuse and can lead to some successful bluffing.

DO SAY: *I thought I'd have a go on a foiling Moth (a hairy single-hander with hydrofoils underneath). Fantastic to fly on a sailboat at 30 knots. After twenty minutes I had a bit of trouble on a gybe and managed to twist my knee, so I'm off games till the cruciate is fixed. But let me tell you how the foils work – a wand adjusts the angle of the front foil automatically and you twist the tiller extension to alter the pitch of the one on the rudder...*

You won't have a clue what you're talking about and neither will they, but eventually their eyes will glaze over – giving you the chance shut up and accept their good wishes and another beer.

DON'T SAY: *I slipped on the launching ramp and landed heavily on my coccyx. Sadly, sailing is a sport where you have to sit for long periods...*

3. Altruism

This is your chance to demonstrate your empathy and self-restraint in turning down the invitation to crew their Tolpuddle One Design next Sunday.

DO SAY: *I'd love to, but sadly I have a three-line whip on (choose one of the following):*

- *taking my grandmother to her kitesurfing lesson*
- *supporting my teenage son while he has, like, his lobotomy*
- *dressing in pink and ferrying my granddaughter to spend her tooth-fairy money*

- *practising as the rear end of a pantomime horse for next week's fancy dress ball.*

DON'T SAY: *Sadly I've responded to the Commodore's request to re-plumb the toilet block that weekend. So while you're sailing I could literally be round the bend.*

4. The Proud Owner Syndrome

If you're feeling particularly intrepid, you could mention that you have your own yacht.

DO SAY: *It's so tempting to come on your annual cruise but, sadly, most of my sailing time is on my Swan 65. I need to go down most months, otherwise the crew start treating her like their own boat. You'd be amazed what I find if I drop in unexpectedly...*

DON'T SAY: *After spending years slumming it on tiny boats I'm afraid I don't sail on anything less than 50 feet.*

When bluffing doesn't work

It's not often that bluffing fails, but occasionally you may find yourself reluctantly afloat. As your skill level is probably slightly lower than a pygmy at a skyscraper convention, this has enormous potential for disaster. So what can you do to mitigate loss of face or, worse, be exposed as a shameless bluffer?

As a good strategy, anything legal you can do *before* the wet stuff hits you is a bonus:

Carry A Basic Rescue Kit

A chandler will sell you a few metres of rope and some

shackles to keep in your pocket, to be retrieved at strategic moments to help a struggling skipper.

Check The Forecast
This can't be over-stressed. Look up the wind forecast on the web (search windguru or xcweather) and the time of high tide (search easytide).

Prepared with this you can sound knowledgeable as you step aboard, before scuttling below asap to avoid being rumbled.

Forestall A Mutiny
Also find out the skipper's favourite tipple and pack a bottle in your kitbag. Most skippers start behaving like Captain Bligh as soon as they get on a boat, so a quick drink might calm things down, may delay a mutiny and will make the point that you and the skipper do think alike in one area at least. By the time the bottle is empty, and the skipper is dozing fitfully, you may even be able to delay your departure and steal away silently.

Wear A Lifejacket
Of course it's a good idea to be able to swim. But in case you can't, or might forget in the heat of the moment, it's best to wear a lifejacket. If it's a foam flotation aid you can wear it under your jacket to look hunky. But if it's the type that inflates on immersion, wear it outside your anorak or you may find that if it blows up inside your jacket and the pressure stops you breating. You don't want to end your days looking like a small airship.

Dress Appropriately

Further planning will depend on whether you're going on a yacht or a dinghy. Dinghy sailing is wetter but only lasts a couple of hours. Yacht cruising should be drier but can go on for days.

On a yacht you'll need to keep the spray and rain at bay so take wellies (call them seaboots) and waterproofs (oilies). You'll also need a sleeping bag and, possibly, a pillow and a towel. Pack a torch so you can find your way to the loo (the heads) in the night. You can also gain brownie points by holding it (the torch) while the skipper tries to fix the engine in the dark.

Know The Ropes

Ropework is important because as soon as you get on board you will find yourself undoing the mooring lines (casting off), untying fenders and so on. So check in a book how to cleat a rope, coil it and throw one end to someone ashore. (Your neighbours will enjoy it if you practise this in the garden.) You will also meet a wide range of knots on the boat. There are 3,800 knots in the definitive *Ashley's Book of Knots* but the bluffer can probably get away with just one, and the best is the Round Turn and Two Half Hitches. It can cope with most jobs on a boat and will also be useful ashore for restraining fleeing crew members.

First steps afloat

You may also like to practise getting on and off a yacht, since this is the first thing you'll do in front of your new crewmates. You want to step up onto the gunwale (the edge of the deck) holding the shroud (the wire that holds up the mast). Do this with each leg. Then, still holding the shroud, swing one leg then the other over the guardrail (the horizontal wires that go round the deck to prevent people falling off). To get off, hold the shroud and swing one leg then the other over the guardrail and onto the gunwale, then step down one leg at a time onto the dock. DON'T get caught trying to step straight over the guardrail with one foot on the dock and the other on the deck, or you'll finish up with the wire between your legs (confirming your bluffer status and resulting in a nasty wedgie situation).

Alternatively you may find yourself crewing a dinghy as opposed to a yacht. Dinghy sailors love getting cold and wet but as a bluffer make sure you have a warm hat, gloves, neoprene boots and a wetsuit.

Sailing a dinghy is a bit more up-close-and-personal as you'll be virtually sitting on the helmsman's lap, making it hard to cover your mistakes. Ward off future criticism by bluffing that most of your sailing has been in single-handers (one-man boats, such as the Laser dinghy). These don't have a jib (the little sail at the front) or a spinnaker (a big coloured extra sail) or – heaven forbid – a trapeze (a wire from the mast which clips to the crew's harness, allowing him to stand out from the side of the boat for more leverage). So when, later, you're swinging round the forestay like a demented acrobat with your jib flapping and the spinnaker wrapped round the rudder you can mention that you never had these problems at the Laser Worlds.

If your helmsman insists on racing suggest a few tacks and gybes (turns) on the way out to the start. Have a go at hoisting, gybing and lowering the spinnaker and, after the inevitable cock-ups, suggest that it 'might be faster' to simply leave it in the bag during the race. If he's got any sense he'll agree, and you're off the hook.

Finally, whether you're cruising or racing, try not to do anything too well (no problem for the bluffer). Otherwise, heaven forbid, you might be asked back, and the excuses mentioned above might not be enough to save you.

Chapter 7

CRUISING

If you are reading this chapter you presumably intend to bluff yourself onto a cruising yacht. In your imagination you will be sailing from anchorage to anchorage on a sleek craft manned by beautiful and engaging young people under the direction of a benign skipper. The sun will be out, the tide will be with you and Rod Stewart will be singing *We are Sailing* from the cockpit speakers. Life will be good and you may be seriously thinking of ditching your chartered accountancy practice, job, course or internship.

There was once, very possibly, a day like this but it was in 1982 and shortly afterwards the keel fell off. The Trade Descriptions Act doesn't really apply to cruising.

Part of cruising's charm is that the unexpected can happen at any moment. So if you have a character which allows you to enjoy hardship and disappointment while attempting to get from A to B at less than five knots, read on. Otherwise you'd be best to try bluffing yourself onto a racing yacht or, heaven forbid, even a dinghy.

Cruising is a surprisingly complex and demanding business. On a cruising boat you may be away from land for days. So, as a crew member, you will be expected not only to sail but to tackle some of the jobs needed to keep the boat functioning and the crew safe and happy. Of these, arguably the most important is cooking, and the bluffer should seize any opportunity to apply for the job and revitalise any previously dormant culinary skills which (you will claim) once won you a place as a finalist on *Masterchef*. Not only will this protect you from uncomfortable exposure to the elements on deck, it will also preclude a humiliating analysis of your non-existent sailing ability by your fellow crew members.

Cooking, key points

There are numerous things to consider if you do decide to spend time in the galley:

- You are down below, warm, dry and near the booze locker.
- You won't get asked to do any dirty jobs (nobody wants the cook to clean the heads before preparing dinner).
- You can start drinking before anyone else. ('I always cook with wine. Sometimes I even put it in the food.')
- After a hard session on deck, sailors are starving and won't be too fussy about what you serve up.
- The cook doesn't usually wash up.
- At sea you will have to make do with the ingredients provided, many of which are way past their sail-by-dates. So if you are planning to be the cook, think ahead and insist on getting food from the supermarket yourself. For maximum bluffing points buy some ready-made stew and bring it aboard in an unmarked dish, claiming that you have been marinading it for days because you feel the

crew 'deserve something wholesome and nutritious at sea – and possibly even digestible.'

- Be sure to bring a sharp knife (the one on board will have been used for cutting rope and even wire) and a non-stick frying pan.

- You may start to feel seasick in the galley because you can't see the horizon. Take some seasickness pills in good time and keep poking your head out of the main hatch to catch a breath of fresh air. If challenged, bluff that you're just waiting for the soup to warm up. If the worst comes to the worst, try not to be sick into the soup pan.

- Beware chopping onions and inhaling spicy stuff in the confines of the galley. Pass up the smelly jobs to the people in the cockpit, pointing out that cooking is a team effort.

If your cooking skills are questionable select a simple cookbook, preferably with waterproof pages. There is a good one with a chapter for each wind strength, i.e. Chapter 1 for Force 1, and so on. Needless to say it's called *The Beaufort Scale Cookbook*. Try not to be seen consulting it too often.

If you get fed up with your cooking role, try a reverse bluff. This implies you're not a strapping jolly jack tar but someone prone to a gastro hissy fit: ('Really! I simply can't cook without coriander, turmeric and juniper berries. And we must anchor within reach of a deli every night.') You're clearly going to be a pain in the neck, so this should do the trick. If all else fails, remember that poisoning the crew is always an option.

Passage making

The skipper should call a crew meeting to explain the passage plan for getting from A to B, and this is the chance for a bluffer to shine.

Check the chart so that you can mention which harbours might serve as boltholes along the way and calculate how long the trip will take – estimating your speed at 5 knots (quick calculation for a bluffer: 1 knot = 1.15 miles per hour) so you can bag the best watches.

Everyone now dons oilskins, lifejackets and harnesses, takes them off again to go to the heads, gets dressed again, downs some motion sickness pills and texts their last farewells. Then the fun-filled hours at sea can begin.

On watch

A system of watches ensures there are always two people on deck (in case one falls off). You're usually on watch for two hours and can then go below for a couple of hours to sleep.

It's at night that all those hours you've spent clubbing finally pay off. You can justifiably point out that your resilience on the dance floor between 3 and 5am means the crew can sleep easy in their bunks while you guide their little ship safely across the ocean. Reassure them that if anything looks like it's going wrong, you will call all hands on deck (though this will prove less than popular if you are telling them there's a huge ship on a collision course, which turns out to be the island of Sicily 30 miles away).

Another point is that it's easy to get confused in the middle of the night. On a cross-channel crossing to Cherbourg crewman Mike Smith was on watch and called everyone up at 4am announcing 'We're there!' This was a surprise since they'd only been at sea for about six hours. Nevertheless, a bottle of red wine was opened and the celebrations continued until the yacht entered the harbour where a sign read 'Welcome to Brighton Marina'. Somehow Mike had managed to turn the boat through 180 degrees in the night and head back to England. Instead of wine and oysters in France the crew had beer and chips in Brighton and Mike has been known ever since as Vasco da Smith, after the famous navigator.

Seasickness

During seasickness you pass through three stages:

• First, you turn green
• Second, you feel you're going to die
• Third, you're afraid you won't

Now is not the time to regret the cheap rot-gut brandies you downed in port last night. Scan the horizon and to do something to take your mind off the hollow feeling under your tongue. For example, you might speculate on the merits of building a tower halfway across The Channel, where seasick crew could pay to get off the boat, so they are stationary for a few golden hours. Invite estimates on how much people would be willing to pay – let's face it, at that point sufferers aren't in any state to bargain.

If all else fails, be sick *into a bucket*. Although it's tempting to be polite and chunder over the side, you can easily follow your breakfast overboard. As you disappear your crewmates may try to grab your wellies but that may not save you, especially if you have been sensible and bought them a size too big 'so you can kick them off if you fall overboard.' This is irony in action.

At the end of the passage resist the urge to jump ashore and head for the nearest bus stop. Your queasiness will subside as soon as the mooring lines are on, the mess will soon be cleared up and you can join in making plans for the evening's entertainment.

Of course all this can be obviated by taking your seasickness pills in plenty of time. Ask your pharmacist what works best, because nothing gives the game of a bluffer away more entertainingly than a projectile chunder into a bucket.

Rules of the road

The formal title is *The International Regulations for Preventing Collisions at Sea*, usually shortened to the *COLREGS* (admittedly, as acronyms go, it could be better). The rules are long and complex because sailors are forever finding new ways of colliding with anything that floats, e.g. large ships, surfacing submarines, seaplanes coming in to land or long distance swimmers.

While it's a good idea not to bump into another vessel, you'll find your shipmates love to discuss the finer points of the rules, particularly when conversation has dried up on a night watch or at anchor. The bluffer needs to be able to join in, and a bit of study can put you ahead of real sailors in this area at least. It might be terribly dull, but it will enhance your bluffing credentials significantly.

Always remember that '*A risk of collision exists if the bearing of another vessel doesn't change*', so like a good crewman you will be keeping an all-round lookout. When you see a ship coming over the horizon gain bluffing points by immediately mentioning it to the others, adding that they can relax because you've got your eye on it. Look ostentatiously at 'the target' through the guardrails and find an object in line with the ship – a stanchion (the post holding up the wire), a piece of tape, anything will do. Over the next few minutes continue to squint along this line and see if the ship stays on it. If the ship moves ahead of it, it will pass ahead – no problem there. If the ship drops behind it, you will pass ahead of the ship. That sounds OK in theory, but do you really want to squeak across the bow of a 60,000-ton tanker doing 20 knots? It might be time to consider changing your speed or course. If the ship stays on your line (if the bearing doesn't change) you are definitely going to hit it unless one of you does something.

That is where the *COLREGS* come in – they tell you who does what and when. A good bluffer will at this point fish out the binoculars and impress the crew by trying to identify the other craft. In the daytime ships have shapes in their rigging: three balls for example means it's aground (remember this as 'a total balls-up'). At night they have special lights, in this case two red lights plus anchor lights. With the almanac in one hand and your binocs in the other you can spend many happy hours arguing about the nature of the opposition you're about to clobber.

Once you know what you're dealing with, refer to the *COLREGS* which list types of vessel in order of priority. As a sailing boat you come about halfway and will be expected to give way to those above you in the list, while having right of way over those lower down. For example, you give way to a dredger, a minesweeper or a fishing boat. But a common-or-garden boat under power, or a seaplane, gives way to you.

> **DO SAY:** *If we slow down now he will certainly pass a mile ahead, and the problem will disappear.*
> **DON'T SAY:** *The QE2 is a power-driven vessel and we have every right to hold our course. He's sure to avoid us...*

The heads

The little room on a boat containing a toilet, shower (if you're lucky) and washbasin is called 'the heads'. The phrase 'two heads are better than one' refers to the fact that nautical loos are always going wrong, and if you have two there is an outside chance that one of them may be working.

Often the problem is caused by too much toilet paper being crammed into the bowl, followed by over-enthusiastic pumping by the operator. The bluffer should under no circumstances offer to unblock the system. If, however, you draw the short straw try the following:

1. Pump like hell. If you're lucky there will be a bang and the blockage will be blown out into the sea, like an *exocet* from a nuclear sub. If you're unlucky the pressure may blow the pipes off the toilet, which is a good moment to pass the job on to someone else.
2. Pour in some drain unblocker. Wait 20 minutes, then repeat Step 1. If ineffective, resist the urge to drink the rest of the unblocker.

If neither of the above work, it's a case of Heads you Win

and you'll have to bring out a new WC on your next trip. If someone asks why you have a small toilet as hand luggage in the overhead locker on a plane, look affronted and inform them that 'A refined sailor always travels with his own thunderbox.' Lavatory humour usually gets a laugh.

No foreplay on the foredeck

This final section is about sex on board. It's included because, despite the lack of privacy on a small boat, nature does sometimes take its course and the bluffer will need to know the ropes if he's not to be left out.

Once the die is cast you will need some privacy. It shouldn't be too hard to find a project on the boat for you and your significant shipmate, and another task ashore for the rest of the crew.

Unless you're an experienced member of The Mile High Club, bypass the heads and head for the forecabin. This gives maximum privacy and, being in the bows, goes up and down a lot on the waves. You may find this motion helpful. As a further plus the ceiling is low, so you can put your feet on it. (Remember to wipe off any footprints before you emerge.)

Further bluffing advice is beyond the scope of this book, so the final steps are now up to you.

Chapter 8

DINGHY RACING

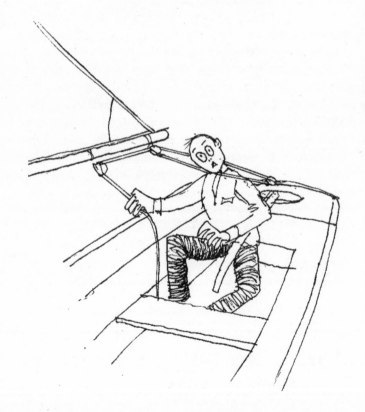

Dinghies are physically demanding to sail and can (and will) capsize. They have the big advantage that you can always stop and go ashore when you've had enough (of the weather, the cold, being shouted at, or coming last).

Dinghies come in classes, e.g. the Laser Class where all the boats are identical (it's a *one design*), or the Merlin Rocket where the class rules allow variation within limits (it's a *development class*).

One designs

Laser sailors believe in the one design principle[2]: since the boats are identical the winner is certainly the best sailor. The only problem is that if you come last, you have no excuse. In the Laser fleet no one talks about having a fast boat, so you will be bluffing about your superior tactics:

This is what you say happened:
'Everyone went right on the second beat but I could see a dark cloud on the left suggesting a windshift. So I went left and sure enough the wind backed over there. I was lifted up to the windward mark and got there miles ahead.'

This is what actually happened:
You decided to take a flier and for once it paid off – the chances of this happening are about 50 :1.

---

[2] Strangely although there is only one design, it has two names: the Laser and the ILCA. Exactly how this came about would need a lawyer (i.e. someone who is paid to bluff) to explain and should not be attempted by the amateur bluffer.

Development classes

In a development class like the Merlin you certainly need to be good to win, but you can improve your chances by experimenting with a new hull or sail design, or by setting up the rig and control lines differently. In the bar Merlin sailors do bluff about tactics, but also about their boats:

This is what you say happened:
'We decided to build her with a fine bow and a flat run aft and were able to move back and plane earlier than everyone else. It gave us 200 yards on every reaching leg.'

This is what actually happened:
You and your helmsman are so light that in Force 2-3 you'd take off downwind in any old tub. But in a proper breeze you'll always struggle with your lack of weight.

The Dinghy Show (for those bluffing in the UK)

This is a good place to get started. It is a wonderful collection of stands, manned by enthusiastic amateurs all eager to get you to join their class or their sailing club. All will tell you their class is definitely the right one for you to sail, e.g. 'Yes, the Higginbottom One Design is perfect for a beginner, you'll soon get used to launching with the boat on its side, wading it out to shoulder depth, then water-starting. And once the foils kick in the boat rises a metre out of the water and flies at 20 knots. It's a great way to learn.'

As a bluffer yourself, you won't be taken in by this. Go round each stand until you become clear which is the best class for you. Then you can use the rest of the day finding out the foibles of the boat. Indeed, the stand will often have the national champion there with *his* boat, only too eager to answer your questions.

Although your truthful opening would be along the lines of: 'Hi, I haven't done much sailing and am new to the class. What's the best way for an unfit, middle aged and penniless sailor to get to the front of your fleet?', with your well-honed bluffing skills, you would be smarter than that. Strike up a rapport, then continue: 'I've done a lot of winning on the Moth circuit but reckon I need a change. Can you tell me a bit about your boats? For instance, I'm fascinated to see the way you can adjust the mast rake while out on the trapeze...' With a bit of luck you'll get all the lowdown on which second hand boat to buy, how to set up the rig, how to tune the wretched thing and how to sail it fast. It would take at least a season to figure out this stuff on your own.

Sailing courses

Once you've found a boat you like the look of, you may decide you need help with your actual sailing. And the Dinghy Show is a good place to research that, too.

If you measure success by the number of Olympic medals, Great Britain is the top sailing nation. If your aim is to become an Olympian, all you need is a dozen or so years of intense training, plenty of raw talent and a killer instinct on the racecourse.

But if you fall into the other 99.9% of the population, the sailing courses available will get you up to a standard where you can enjoy your racing and know enough to bluff with the hotshots when you encounter them at the bar.

Capsizing

A key part of any course is how to handle a capsize, which is inevitable sooner rather than later. If you're quick you may be able to turn around as the boat goes over, clamber over the side and onto the centreboard, lever the boat back upright and slide back in without even getting wet. Simple really. If you're slow you'll probably fall out.

Can't get it up

Then the procedure is as follows (assuming you're in a single-hander):

1. Let go of the tiller extension or it may snap as you go overboard.
2. Hang on to the sheet. Then you are at least connected to the boat.
3. Swim round to the bottom of the boat and pull down on the centreboard. (If you're light you may have to climb onto it to right the boat.)
4. As she comes up swim her around so she's pointing at about 30 degrees to the wind.
5. Reach in and grab the toestrap. Pull yourself into the boat.
6. Pant a lot.

Extra bluffing points: You might like to let slip that you are a bit of an expert at the San Francisco Roll. This happens when you are righting the boat OK but the wind gets behind the sail and flips it over on top of you. Hang onto the centreboard so you are pulled under the water and up on the other side. You can then right the boat with the wind coming from the right direction.

'However,' you might continue, 'on this occasion I was hanging onto the centreboard but the boat came upright and sailed off with me underneath. After a bit I needed to breathe so tried sucking air down the self-bailer, but unfortunately the valve wouldn't open. In the end I had to let go of the centreboard but then the rudder hit me on the head as it went by. The boat sailed some distance before it capsized again; it was a long swim to catch it and the competition reached past showing no sympathy whatsoever. Nowadays I always wear a hard hat and hang on to the mainsheet...'

String-driven thing

If you've made the brave decision to buy a brand new dinghy, when it arrives it will appear to have been fitted out by a *tricoteuse*[3]. Admittedly there won't be guillotined heads lying about, but the deck will look like it's covered in knitting. On closer inspection this turns out to be innumerable control lines and your first job is to pull them one at a time and see what they do. It helps if the ropes are different colours, so the helmsman can show off by yelling 'Trim the starboard twinning line!' then whisper 'Pull the pink one, you clot' so you know what he's on about.

If your boat has a spinnaker do take advice on how to rig it. And, just to be sure, always check by pulling it up in the dinghy park before you go afloat. There's nothing the fleet enjoys more than someone hoisting the kite upside-down. Don't let that someone be you.

The trapeze

If the boat has a trapeze it's worth practising ashore. Chock the boat carefully then get in her, clip on and go out *front foot first*. Keep this front leg braced or you'll swing forward round the forestay like a rag doll.

When you've established equilibrium come back in, cross the boat and go out on the other side. Finally, repeat all this with the jib up as, later, you'll need to control both the jibsheet and the trapeze when you tack. Clear enough?

[3] As a bluffer you will obviously say you know what this word means, but, in case you don't, these were the supportive ladies who knitted while watching the guillotine do its business during the French Revolution.

A good bluff at this stage is to recount how you were scorching along on the trapeze with the spinnaker up in a good blow. The helmsman was also hiked right out to stop the boat capsizing. The reservoir dam was approaching fast so he yelled at you to get the kite down smartish. To do that you'd have needed to come into the boat causing it to capsize, so you told *him* to pull it down. He maintained he couldn't move or the boat *would* go over. This exchange went on until the dinghy really was about to hit the dam, and the only way you could think of stopping was to capsize and pull the spinnaker down at leisure with the boat on her side. You drew three conclusions from this:

1. If you angle your front foot a bit the bow-wave squirts nicely off it into the helmsman's face, which at least shuts him up.
2. If the helmsman had borne away onto a run the boat would have stopped heeling. Then you both could have come in and dropped the spinnaker – before you jeopardised the town's water supply by ramming the dam.
3. Beware the nut on the end of the tiller. In other words, you need to choose your helmsman carefully, then learn to communicate with him – or you'll spend more time swimming than sailing.

Racing

After all this groundwork you are at last ready for your first race. This will probably be a club race: open meetings, championships and the Olympics will have to wait.

Firstly, check the course. The race will be from a start

line, round several buoys, then through the finish line. It is a classic mistake to sail the wrong course so write down the buoys in order on the deck with a chinagraph pencil.

The start is the fun bit, because it's the only time the whole fleet is together. Start your stopwatch at the 5-minute signal, then check it at the 4- and 1-minute signals. Sit near the line with your sails flapping for the final 90 seconds, getting ready for the starting hooter. Your aim is to cross the line just after the start signal, going at full speed.

After that it's a simple matter of sailing round the course as fast as you can, avoiding physical contact with the other boats by shouting at them a lot. Useful expressions include 'Starboard!', 'Windward boat!', 'Water please!', and 'Look out you idiot...' If you do collide with someone else, resist the urge to deck them. Instead shout 'Protest' (see below), push them off, do two penalty turns and resume the race. The messy details of insurance claims and who was in the wrong can be sorted out later, ashore.

The racing rules

Sailing is unusual in having two sets of rules: the *Collision Regulations* for cruising (see page 74) and the *Racing Rules of Sailing* for racing.

Although racing essentially consists of sailing faster than anyone else, over time the regulations have stretched to over 90 Rules as sailors have found ever more ingenious ways to improve their results. These are shrouded in arcane language, with words like 'overlap', 'mark room' and 'redress' appearing throughout. Plus, for even more obfuscation, there are scores of Appeals available, detailing the rule interpretations of really complex cases.

Despite this, sailors love to spin out the pleasure of the race for a few hours by discussing some complicated rule technicality and the bluffer needs to be able to join in. And naturally a good knowledge of the small print can also be a race winner out on the course. So it's recommended that you do a bit of mugging up – after all, this is one of the few ways the bluffer can beat a proper sailor.

It's essential to know the *Rules for When Boats Meet*: in short you'd better watch out if you are:

- A port tack boat (port gives way to starboard)
- A windward boat (windward gives way to leeward)
- Overlapped by another boat approaching a mark (the outside one gives the other room)
- Tacking or altering course (boats not turning have right of way)
- Hailed for room to avoid an obstruction like the shore or the QE2 (you need to give the other dinghy room to tack)

Another area the bluffer should study is outlined in Rule 42, Propulsion. This says you can only propel the boat by the natural action of the wind on the sails and the water on the hull. This is to prevent competitors fanning the boat along faster by rocking her back and forth, repeatedly pulling in the sheets hard, ooching by suddenly moving their bodies forward, sculling by waggling the tiller from side to side, and repeatedly tacking or gybing. Watching any top level fleet will show you exactly how to do this.

You might imagine that sailing races are conducted in silence, but this is far from the truth. Apart from continual shouts of 'Starboard!', 'Hold your course!' and so on, there are plenty of opportunities to sledge, and classics such as the following can be deadly:

- *'Do you know you've got weed on your rudder?'* Weed is every sailor's nightmare; it really slows the boat down. Your victim's only solution is to move aft, lift the rudder and get the weed off. Leaving you to nip by to windward.
- *'Did you go round that last buoy the right way?'* Psychologically damaging; for some reason it's hard to remember. The other crew will have to consult their course list, discuss it and, if they were wrong, go back and round it the right way. You will be long gone...
- *'I think you may be in breach of Appendix E, Rule 4.2 (b).'* They won't have a clue what this is. Neither will you, since it's actually one of the rules for radio-controlled model boat racing. But it sounds like you mean business and may spook them long enough for you to get past.
- *'Your mainsail is hoisted above the black band.'* You could protest them on this and by the time they've slackened off the control lines, unravelled the halyard and lowered the sail a couple of inches you'll be ahead of them.

Judgement Day

Sailing is also unusual in that there is (mostly) no referee: the sailors police themselves. If you think you're in the wrong you are expected to do two 360 degree turns, which puts you back a bit but exonerates you. If neither party does turns then there is a protest afterwards, which is like a mini court of law with a protest committee (the jury), witnesses called, and so on. At the end there is a verdict, and one boat may be disqualified.

A protest hearing is fertile ground for the bluffer. Indeed, the two parties' descriptions of what happened are usually so dissimilar that they appear to be completely different incidents. Lying about what happened is considered poor form; just use your knowledge of the rules (see below) and try not to sound like someone in a crime series on TV.

> **DO SAY:** *I'm protesting boat 4571 under Rule 10. She approached on port tack, and I was on starboard. My hail of 'Starboard' had no effect and at the last minute I luffed to avoid damage. We touched bow to bow. I immediately called 'Protest'. The incident was witnessed by boat 3689.*
>
> **DON'T SAY:** *4571 was proceeding in a northerly direction with intent to rearrange the gelcoat on my port side. I called starboard but he raised two fingers, hit my boat amidships and punched me in the throat. Her helmsman has only recently been released from a ban for Bringing the Sport into Disrepute for slagging off the commodore's wife. Luckily my crew is in the Flying Squad and talked some sense into him with a taser. I put it to the protest committee that they should lock him up…*

By now, you have doubtless got the message: dinghy racing is effectively a paradise for a bluffer. And so is its big brother, yacht racing.

Chapter 9

YACHT RACING

It's not true that owning a racing yacht is like standing under a cold shower tearing up five pound notes. Rather, it's like walking across Alaska in your boxers while the crew liquidate all your assets.

Now you have a bit of experience you won't, of course, fall for the yacht-owning trap. Better to be a typical crew member and bluff your way into the Crew's Union by relating humorous tales about owners you've sailed with. You'd be wise to have a few of these anecdotes up your sleeve:

Bluff 1: 'In the frenetic pre-start melee of Cowes Week our owner yelled, "Get those oilskins off the foredeck!" Or intended to. Sadly, what came out was "Get those foreskins off the oildeck!" We were laughing so much we couldn't move the oilskins – or the foreskins for that matter.'

Bluff 2: 'Our owner, a knight of the realm, was at the helm of his yacht in a major regatta but had lost concentration. The tactician, keen to avoid a collision, plucked up the courage to speak: "Suggest you bear away, Sir." The owner irritably agreed but turned the wheel the wrong way. The tactician took a deep breath, then, to the crew's amusement, muttered: "Suggest you bear away the other way, Sir."'

Bluff 3: 'Our owner in this instance was a nightmare on board. A know-all, and a hopeless sailor who persistently ignored advice, he'd say: "Don't argue, I'll use the prop walk to bring the stern round", promptly side-swiping another moored boat. Or "I don't believe your forecast. I think Force 9 is a complete exaggeration. We're setting sail." A miserable night at sea for all on board would follow.

But by happy coincidence one of our crew was at a nearby RNLI station for their open day and was looking through the rescue log. And, bingo, there was an entry for our owner calling out the lifeboat to drag him off a local sandbank. Our crewman bided his time to bring it up. Then, a few weeks later, he was being berated for not polishing the fenders properly or something equally idiotic. So he casually mentioned it might be better to spend less time on trivia and more on avoiding catastrophes. There was a gasp from the rest of the crew, but his street cred skyrocketed when he dropped the rescue into the ensuing argument. Game set and match, and we've had no trouble with the owner since.'

But don't get carried away and bluff about your *current* owner. He's paying for the boat and it's he who allocates jobs on board. Plus he's the only one who knows where crucial bits of equipment are stowed – like the liferaft, the first aid kit and the corkscrew. Unless you want to be given the 3am watch every day and be denied the soothing benefits of alcohol, do try to be nice to him. You never know, you might be short of a ride and want to sail on his boat again.

Events for racing yachts are pretty diverse. The bluffer would be well advised to start with a few short, daytime races before moving on to something more ambitious.

Inshore racing

For a quiet life you might simply do the club race every week. This involves turning up in the morning, motoring out to the start then racing round some local buoys before putting the boat away and enjoying a few pints in the bar before noshing a good roast. Nothing wrong with that, particularly if the owner foots the bill.

This idea can be extended by crewing in a regatta such as Cowes Week, where you race for a few hours every day to give you a thirst for your evenings in the beer tent. You may sleep on the yacht, but this still counts as day sailing since you are tied up in the marina at night.

These are inshore races, i.e. you are always in sight of land. They are similar to dinghy racing, and indeed the rules are the same for both. So they are an ideal first step for a dinghy sailor planning his move into yachting.

Offshore racing

Things hot up when the course is longer, and you need to sail overnight. For example, a JOG (Junior Offshore Group) race typically starts on a Friday at 8pm in the Solent and you race across the Channel to a French port like Cherbourg, arriving on Saturday in good time for the Mayor's cocktail party. This usually involves litres of questionable brandy, which you will regret on Sunday morning when you have to sail the yacht back to the Solent. *Mal de mer* follows not long after you start off.

You may like to bluff about your race from Cowes to Saint-Vaast, a popular Normandy destination because it has a world class restaurant called *Les Fuchsias*: 'Before the start of the race on Friday we booked our table for Saturday night, then spent the 85 nautical mile race worrying whether we'd arrive in time. The wind was dropping and we reckoned we might not only miss dinner, we might even fail to get through the last lock into the marina and have to spend the night at anchor, tortured by cooking smells wafting over the water from *Fuchsias*. With 20 miles to go it became clear this was indeed going to happen so the Crew's Union elected me to negotiate with the skipper to abandon the race, turn on the engine and motor like hell for France. Like most skippers he was reluctant to abandon, but gave in when I mentioned the oysters, sole meuniere and ripened Normandy cheeseboard. We made our table with 15 minutes to spare and were cheered to find half the fleet tucking in, having also chosen restaurant over race.'

In case you are beginning to think that offshore sailors lack determination, it's worth mentioning that some races are *much* longer. Knowing about these is a strong weapon for any bluffer to keep in his arsenal, ready to be bragged about on long night watches.

The ARC

The Atlantic Rally for Cruisers is a 3,000-mile race from Las Palmas in the Canaries to St Lucia in the Caribbean. Over 200 assorted yachts make the voyage – for many it's a delivery trip in good company, for others it's a serious race. It takes an average boat about 16 days and they are always full of incident, so the bluffing potential is huge. You might dine out on some of the following casual recollections:

- 'We started with 700 litres of water and 750 litres of diesel, enough for 1,000 miles of motoring. The ARC rules are unusual in that you *are* allowed to motor, but a time penalty is added for each hour under engine. In the end we didn't use much diesel: the wind was mostly a steady Force 6 from astern giving champagne sailing at 8 knots in the Trade Winds.'

- 'News came in frequently from other yachts having difficulties: a rudder fell off, a mast snapped, a crewman fell off. We too had a major emergency – we ran out of marmalade on Day 10. The skipper got a lot of stick for that, and breakfast was a sombre meal for the rest of the race.'

- 'The waves are big in the Atlantic and the boat rolled every 4 seconds. Over 16 days that's 345,000 rolls. Since there were 5 men on board, that's more that 1.5 million man-rolls. This explains why you have to keep a yacht's floor clean – at some stage you'll be eating your lunch off it.'

Dangerous Moonlight

A major feature of offshore racing is that you have to sail at night. Indeed, most races are won by the crew who can keep the speed on through the hours of darkness, when everyone is tired and vision is difficult.

On short offshore races the crew may sit on the rail

all night to provide the maximum righting effect. Take this opportunity of a captive audience for some extended bluffing.

DO SAY (to the helmsman): *We're going great, speed's 6.4 knots and the compass shows we're lifted 5 degrees.*
DON'T SAY: *Could you slow down a bit, the spray's getting us really wet.*

DO SAY (to the navigator): *There's a buoy about 400 yards on the port bow, flashing three times every 10 seconds.*
DON'T SAY: *I know you're dozing off but I've been watching a large ship for ages and it's only a hundred yards away now, doing about 20 knots. I think it's on a collision course.*

On longer races the watch system should be set up to give everyone a chance of some sleep. You will probably need no encouragement to sleep during the day, too. You might recount that during a race in the Caribbean your cabin mate, who snores for Britain, was asleep on the top bunk getting some shuteye before the night watches. The porthole was open which allowed a flying fish to soar through, straight into his mouth. The spluttering was something awful and he refused to believe we hadn't used it as a plug to shut him up – though come to think of it...

The vision problem at night can be partly cured by rigging up lights to shine on the telltales on the sails (strips of wool which show the airflow). Then you can trim the sheets so the telltales stream nicely on both sides of each sail, and if you can do that all night you're halfway to winning.

It will also help if there is a repeater for the instruments. This is usually on the mast and if it's lit at night the whole crew can see the boat's speed, position, distance to waypoint and so on. It's an inclusive idea which encourages everyone to keep working, or at least to stay awake. It's also a useful prompt for some good bluffing, such as:

'Seeing our coordinates reminds me of the time race control called us on the radio and asked the navigator "What's your position?"

"My position? I'm at the chart table."

There was a pause at the other end, then: "Race control again. Your position understood. Any idea of the chart table's lat and long?"'

Other tried and tested anecdotes about offshore racing might include:

- 'I used to sail with a couple of surgeons on their ketch *Cirrhosis of the River*. They always went high on the buoy at this stage because the tide off Cherbourg is really strong. I guess they couldn't risk getting in too late for the run ashore to the booze warehouse.'
- 'A modern navigator has it easy – with the GPS he always knows where the boat is. When I started it was all DR (Dead Reckoning). I remember one race from Cowes to CH1 buoy off Cherbourg and back. We were trimming all

night like crazy, and reckoned we were doing well. There was a tantalising smell of garlic but we just couldn't find CH1 in the dark, and after zig-zagging for an hour had to give up and sail home. With hindsight, maybe we should have gone ashore to try our luck wherever we landed.'

Navigating

Actually the navigator's job is anything but a doddle. Ideally the boat should sail from one buoy to another in as straight a line as possible (the rhumb line), and often the winner is the boat that sails the shortest distance through the water. Unfortunately the tide, wind, shallows and crew limitations combine to modify this objective.

For example, the *tide* is slacker inshore, because of the friction between the water and the land. So it may well pay to deviate from the direct line, going close inshore when sailing against the tide but heading offshore when sailing with it. The question is: How far is it worth deviating? The decision is down to the navigator and his skills at chartwork.

If the tide is running across the course the idea is to aim off a bit so the yacht crabs down the rhumb line. The navigator has to calculate the best course to steer, further complicated by the tide gradually changing in strength and direction over roughly a twelve-hour cycle.

Nor is the *wind* constant. If you are on a beat and the wind is due to veer (shift clockwise) then it will pay to head out to the starboard side of the course, and tack when the windshift arrives. If a back is forecast, go left. Have you got all that? If you can quote any of it, it might convince an impressionable audience that you know what you're talking about – even if they don't understand a word of it (rather like you).

Vitally, you don't want to hit anything along the way, be it rocks, *shallows*, headlands or large ships. That's why the navigator should sleep, if he has time to sleep at all, with a chart on his chest.

Lastly, remember that a yacht can't always point in the direction you'd like. If the wind is ahead you'll have to beat, and the number of tacks it's worth making depends on the *crew's skill*. A spinnaker is trouble waiting to happen so if the wind is behind and strong you may lose a lot on each gybe unless the crew are very competent. Either way, it may pay to sail a little further than risk a foul-up.

Because of the complexity involved it follows that the bluffer should under no circumstances agree to be navigator. The buck stops at the chart table and if you are at the back of the fleet the finger will point at you. It could be the last time anyone will buy you a beer or offer you his sister's (or brother's) phone number. Don't do it! Rather, go all misty, look into the distance and murmur with a catch in your voice '… but for those rocks off Portland Bill… we'd have caught the tide… all the way to the Fastnet… and *Maid of the Mudflat* might still be afloat… and… Twice Nightly Whitely… might still be with us… (choke)…'

With your finely-honed bluffing skills, you should be able to carry it off.

You're much better off as a simple crewman at the front of the cockpit, dry under the sprayhood, casting aspersions on the owner (if he's out of earshot), the course, the helming, the tuning and, indeed, on yacht racing in general. And probably wishing you were on a flotilla holiday in Greece.

Chapter 10
SAILING HOLIDAYS

Before letting you loose on one of their expensive yachts, a sailing holiday company will need some idea of your level of competence. This is probably the only time in this book that we don't recommend a mega-bluff: if your only qualification is Day Skipper Theory (failed) it's probably best to admit it now, before you find yourself losing what's left of your nine lives.

In general there are two types of yachting holiday: *chartering* or joining a *flotilla*. Alternatively, if dinghies are your thing you can try a *dinghy sailing week*.

Chartering

Chartering is just another word for hiring a yacht.

If you're taking the boat without a professional skipper, this is a *bareboat charter* (don't get too excited, nudity is not part of the deal). It follows that you're going to have to do everything yourselves, so it's worth mentioning the skills you simply must have within the crew:

- You must have someone who can handle mooring lines. If you can't throw a rope to a helper ashore, then docking in an offshore wind is going to be a nightmare.

- Getting the sails up and down is relatively straightforward, but you must know how to reef both the genoa and the mainsail. Keep a lookout for wind arriving and reef early to reduce the sail area. If the wind drops don't shake out the reefs too soon: have a cup of tea and see if the wind really has gone down.

- Navigation is important. You need someone who understands a chart or at least realises that you want to stay on the blue bits and avoid anything coloured green. Remind them that hitting a rock at full tilt can ruin your whole day.

- You need a method of getting weather information for the local area such as the internet, VHF radio or Navtex. If you can access it from your bunk so much the better – if the weather is going to be atrocious, you can just turn over and go back to sleep.

- Someone should be able to operate the VHF radio and send an emergency call. This reaches all boats that are in range, but the flip side of this is that no conversation is private.
- Things break and go wrong all the time on a yacht, so someone is going to have to fix them. The main culprits are the engine, the heads and the electrics. So ideally your crew will include a mechanic, a plumber and an electrician. If not, you'll find that many people who have never even banged in a nail seem quite at home in the bowls of the boat changing the engine oil or replacing the toilet pump. This is one of life's mysteries.
- Anchoring is a key skill. You can drop the kedge (the small anchor) for lunch on a calm day or drop the bower (the big one) to hold you at night. Whichever you use, make sure that the inboard end of the chain is firmly attached to a strong point. Otherwise the whole lot may go to the bottom. As exemplified by the following radio exchange between a punter and the charter company:

  'Hello. Can you come over please, we've got a problem. Over.'

  'Can you say what the problem is? Over.'

  'Yes, we need some more anchors. Over.'

  'But you've got two on board. Over.'

  'No, we've used both of those. And there's five more days to go…'
- Lastly, have a few games up your sleeve to keep the crew happy when a trip gets boring. If it's sunny and everyone is in swimming togs, rig up a plank across the foredeck and out over the water and see who can 'walk the plank'

to the end. You'll be surprised how difficult this is, and watching other people fall in the water always raises the spirits.

Flotilla sailing

A flotilla is a group of yachts – usually 2- to 6-berth sloops between 28 and 40 feet long – that sail together and are headed by a lead yacht with a professional crew. They are trained to spot a bluffer, so be on your guard.

Each day starts with a briefing on the day's route, the weather and anything interesting along the way. The yachts then sail together or separately to the same destination and tie up. The lead boat usually arrives first and helps the yachts moor together.

A pecking order will gradually develop among the sailors, and it's essential that the bluffer emerges at the head of the pack. Since your sailing is suspect, aim to shine in the evening: make sure you have plenty of booze on board and can generate loud music and yours will become the go-to boat for preprandials.

It's fun to see how low in the water a yacht becomes as more people pile on deck, entertaining to heel her by all moving to one side, and hilarious to watch the pontoon become awash as they all stand on it. But a wise bluffer knows his limitations, so head ashore for dinner before you reach the irresistible stage, or actually damage the yacht. You do have to sail her tomorrow.

Mooring Stern-To

Many flotillas sail in non-tidal waters where the form is

to moor at right angles to the jetty, with the stern almost touching it. You then extend a plank from the boat to the bank and walk ashore.

The tricky bit is getting the yacht into this position in the first place.

This is what should happen:
1. While well off the dock prepare a long stern line on both the port and starboard sides.
2. Lower fenders on both sides of the yacht.
3. Get the anchor ready at the bow.
4. Explain what each person is going to do.
5. Choose your target spot on the jetty and try to encourage someone ashore to stand there to take your lines.
6. Reverse towards the target at a reasonable speed.
7. When you're three or four lengths away, drop the anchor and let the chain run freely as the boat reverses in.
8. As the stern approaches the dock slow down and 'check' the anchor chain. The boat will stop.
9. Throw the stern lines to the helpers ashore. They should cleat them either side.
10. Adjust the stern lines and the anchor cable to hold the boat firmly just off the jetty.
11. Set up the plank and send someone across it to bring back cold beer from the taverna.

This is what does happen:
1. The boat motors in too slowly and a crosswind blows her

sideways onto the next yacht.

2. The helmsman panics, puts the throttle the wrong way and rams the dock.

3. The helper ashore is nautically challenged and fails to catch either shore line, then falls in trying to retrieve them.

4. Your anchor drags as the strain comes on it, so you have to go out and start again. (But your anchor line is twisted around other anchor lines, so you can't.)

The Yacht's Dinghy

On flotilla you will use the dinghy a lot more than you would in home waters. A dinghy in use is a good, practical way of getting ashore. Otherwise, the dinghy is a pain in the neck. Where are you going to put the wretched thing? You could inflate and deflate it every time, but this is tedious. You could tow it, but this slows you down. If there's any wind it'll skit about and may even flip over. (You can prevent this problem by putting your most loquacious crewman in it and letting out the towrope to its full extent.) You could lash it onto the foredeck, but it really gets in the way there (think bouncy castle in a small living room). Or you could pull it up the stern of the yacht and tie it to the backstay. This does get it out of the way but blocks the view astern – just when you should be keeping a lookout for large, overtaking ships.

Dinghy sailing holidays

At the end of a long winter why not kick off the new season with some dinghy sailing in the sun? If you choose carefully you should be able to find a venue with (almost) guaranteed wind, teaching for beginners and racing for the more experienced. You can try lots of dinghy classes and maybe have a go at windsurfing and SUP (Stand Up Paddleboarding).

Lasers

230,000 sailors can't be wrong – the Laser is a wonderful boat. Start your holiday on one of these, choosing a rig (4.7, Radial or Standard – or ILCA 4, ILCA 6 or ILCA 7 in new money) to suit your experience.

The holiday staff will rig and launch the boat for you (don't get too used to this luxury) and push you off. Lower the rudder, push down the daggerboard, and sail away. Reach up and down a bit to get the feel of the boat; tack facing forwards and only change hands on the sheet and tiller after you have settled on the new side of the boat. Once you feel confident try a beat to windward, a run and a gybe. Now you're really flaunting it!

All boats have their quirks and the Laser's is that the sheet can catch round the back (strictly the quarter) of the hull. You can score some good bluffing points by telling your listeners that this is caused by the sheet being too slack – it then falls into the water, is washed aft in the boat's wake and catches round the stern when it's tensioned again. Continue thus: 'To prevent this I always wind in the sheet as I tack. For gybing I get going flat out, pull in an armful of sheet, heel the boat to windward (to lift the sheet up, away from the water) and give the sheet a tug as I turn. In one flowing movement, naturally.'

Of course this is pure bluff and, if you are not to be

rumbled, you'll need to go out behind an island and practise. A couple of days should do it, and after that you'll *need* a holiday.

The only other danger point for the bluffer is landing, particularly on a lee shore (the wind blowing onto the shore). Here the Laser is brilliant – you simply untie the knot in the end of the mainsheet, let the rig blow downwind like a flag, and drift ashore – pulling up the daggerboard and rudder just before they hit the bottom. Don't forget to drop the details of this technique into the conversation later, for extra bluffing points.

Other Dinghies

Some companies offer you the chance to sail a Waszp. This is also a single-hander but with wings to sit out on and foils underneath to lift the boat out of the water. The best advice has always been that you shouldn't sail anything you can't spell. And even if you can, it's not a boat for the bluffer. And if you do bluff yourself onto one, make sure you wear a crash helmet.

You may also be offered two-man boats to sail, and this is a good idea since you'll have someone else to blame. Alternatively, take one of the instructors with you 'just to polish up your more advanced skills.' Get them to show you how to handle an asymmetric spinnaker, for serious bluffing later: 'So much easier than a conventional kite. You pull one string and the pole goes out and the sail up at the same time. To gybe you just pull it round with the sheet, like a big jib. And you pull it down with a retrieval line. The only real problem is what angles to sail downwind.'

Windsurfers

On a windsurfer you use the wind to reach, run, beat, tack and gybe. So far so good, you have mastered these evolutions in your dinghy sailing. But in other ways windsurfing is a new sport because you sail standing up, lean the rig to windward to balance the wind, and have no rudder or sheet.

The cleverest bit of a windsurfer is the universal joint (UJ) at the foot of the mast. It lets you rock the rig forward (which pushes the bow away from the wind) or aft (which pushes the stern away from the wind). This is how you steer.

The UJ also allows you to lean the mast (and yourself) to windward: your weight hanging down balances the force of the wind on the sail and powers the board forwards.

The wishbone is a bit like the boom on a dinghy. Since you have no sheet you pull the wishbone towards you to pull in the sail, and let it rotate away from you to ease the sail.

Windsurfing is simply (!) a matter of adjusting these three elements individually – a bit like rubbing your stomach and tapping your head at the same time.

Now let's get the board sailing. Uphaul the rig out of the water. Lean the rig forward or aft until the board is aligned across the wind. LEAN BACK while pulling in the wishbone until everything is in balance. And off you go. If you want to turn into the wind rake the rig back a bit and pull in the wishbone a little. Once you are on course, go back to the original rake. If a gust hits ease out the wishbone, which allows you to lean back a bit more, then pull in the wishbone to its original position.

And so it goes.

Once ashore, don your Bermuda shorts and '*Windsurfers*

Do It Standing Up' T-shirt and head for the bar. For good bluffing points go through in detail that whopper wave your rode in: 'I headed inshore in a trough, bore away and carved back off the top of the white water down the face. After working the wave to the max I duck gybed and sailed out through what was left of the wave. That wave doesn't trouble me anymore.' It helps if you have blonde hair and speak with a Californian accent, but do your best.

If challenged, switch the conversation to something you do understand, or fall back on that tried and tested prop used by any good bluffer, The Rant. This is pretty easy as windsurfers have plenty to be cranky about. They can't have any fun unless it's blowing Force 4 or above. However fast they sail, there's always someone faster (the fastest speed for a windsurfer is about 60mph). And the cool guys have terrific names like Robby Swift, Antoine Albeau or Bjorn Dunkerbeck. What chance does a Pete Smith stand?

Stand Up Paddleboarding

SUP is the new kid on the block. Strictly, of course, it's not sailing, but it's the fastest-growing watersport in the world, and many holiday companies will have boards for you to try – and we are trying to make this book popular.

Compared with sailing, it's not too hard. Climb on the board. Move to the middle and stand up with your feet either side of the handle. Face forwards. Hold the paddle with your hands shoulder-width apart. Rotate your shoulders so the paddle moves forward and put it in the water with the shaft vertical. Pull the paddle back through the water. Lift the paddle up when it gets near your feet. And repeat.

If you're paddling on the left you may find the board turns right, so switch to paddling on the right to straighten up. But it's better to go straight in the first place: make sure you're taking short strokes with a vertical shaft and turn the blade slightly so it directs water under the board. That should do it!

At the bar the bluffer might mention a couple of paddleboarding cracker jokes:

- 'How do paddleboarders avoid constipation?' 'They use SUPpositories.'
- 'How do paddleboarders greet each other?' 'They say "What's SUP."'

A groan is the right response...

Chapter 11

ADVANCED BLUFFING

Up to this point most of the recommended bluffing has been of a practical nature. But you also need to be prepared to shine during, say, a wet afternoon in the sailing club. So here are a few key facts about some of the most prominent names and boats in the history of sailing to drop into the conversation.

Slocum

Captain Joshua Slocum, a much-travelled American seafarer, was the first man to sail alone around the world. He did this in *Spray*, a boat which had been left to rot in a field. Slocum was given it, then spent 3 years rebuilding her with his own hands, for example cutting down an oak tree from which he made the keel. He lengthened her to 37 feet and altered her to a more sea-kindly shape. She weighed 9 tons.

He set off on 24 April, 1895 from Boston, aged 51, and sailed 46,000 miles alone, arriving back in Newport, Rhode Island, nearly three years later, without the benefit of GPS or Navtex. His route was west-about, although he first sailed to Gibraltar, then back across the Atlantic to Brazil, then via the Straits of Magellan (Cape Horn) to Australia, then back via the Cape of Good Hope. He often stopped en route, sometimes for several weeks. He was welcomed in each port and often asked to give a lecture, which he used to raise money to pay for food and repairs.

In 1909 he set out for one more voyage in the *Spray* but was never seen again. Too good a sailor to have foundered, it's believed he was run down in the night by a ship. Luckily he lives on in his classic book, *Sailing Alone Around the World*, published in 1900.

Joshua Slocum and Spray

Key Bluffing Points
- Slocum never learnt to swim, adopting the principle that you're safer *on* the water than *in* it.
- In the Straits of Magellan he was concerned that the savages who had been following him in their canoes would board him at night, so he sprinkled the deck with tin tacks. At midnight the barefoot savages did attack but 'howled like a pack of hounds' on treading on the tacks and jumped overboard, with Slocum firing several shots

into the dark.

- The *Spray* was beautifully balanced: he once set the wheel and then sailed 2,000 miles across the Pacific without touching the helm again. He mostly spent the time reading.
- He had an argument with President Kruger of South Africa, who said that, since the world is flat, he should say he is sailing on it, not round it. Slocum's voyage clearly clinched his argument.

Knox-Johnston

Sir Robin Knox-Johnston is the first person to sail around the world *non-stop*, single-handed.

He left Falmouth on 14 June 1968, aged 29, and circled the world east-about. He logged 30,123 nautical miles in 313 continuous days at sea, at an average speed of 4.02 knots. He arrived back in Falmouth ten months later, on 22 April 1962, to a tumultuous welcome and the steak, hot bath, pint of beer and clean white sheets he had been dreaming of.

His boat, the ketch *Suhaili*, was built of teak in India. She was only 32ft long but had a canoe stern, enabling her to cope with the huge waves in the Southern Ocean. Although the hull was tough, the gear gradually crumbled: at the halfway point his water tanks were polluted, the self-steering had failed as had the radio transmitter and the engine. Plus the sails were taking a pounding: he now spent much of his time steering and sewing and gathering rainwater. The loss of the radio meant that his only contact was when sighted from the shore or if he could attract the attention of a passing ship. This meant that, to the outside world, he was 'lost' for most of the voyage.

Nonetheless he completed the voyage and, amazingly, completed another circumnavigation in 2007 at the age of 68 in a boat appropriately sponsored by Saga.

Robin Knox-Johnston and Suhaili

Key Bluffing Points
- To feed himself Sir Robin (knighted in 1995) took 1,500 tins of food, varnished to stop them rusting (including 226 tins of corned beef and 144 of stewing steak). These, plus fresh food, dehydrated rations and a case of brandy, another of Scotch, 120 cans of lager and 3,000 cigarettes, weighed over a ton.
- He made each bottle of hooch last 16 days, on average. He didn't run out of food but did get through all the ciggies.
- While repairing the spinnaker in the saloon in a rough sea he managed to sew his moustache to the sail.
- He picked his departure date so as to round Cape Horn in

January. Apparently this is the safest time, though calling Cape Horn 'safe' is rather like claiming Ghengis Khan was 'unassuming'.

- When he returned he was asked what it was like to be lost for so long. He replied that he was never lost – he knew exactly where he was.

Crowhurst

Donald Crowhurst has to be the archetypal bluffer (even if his is a profoundly cautionary tale). He entered the 1968/69 Golden Globe singlehanded round the world race in *Teignmouth Electron*, a trimaran built in just 5 months and launched well before she was seaworthy.

In the event she only got as far as South America where Crowhurst stopped but sent a series of bluffing reports of his progress as though he was continuing the race. His plan was to wait until the competitors came past him on their way to the finish, join in again and finish in a respectable position. However it seems likely that the realisation gradually dawned on him that his race would soon come under the microscope and his bluff would be called.

Donald Crowhurst and Teignmouth Electron

No-one knows what he did next, but sometime later *Teignmouth Electron* was found adrift with no sign of Crowhurst. His logbooks were still on board and, judging from the increasingly bizarre entries, it seems possible that he threw himself overboard to avoid ridicule and bankruptcy.

Key Bluffing Points
- Ironically, the other trimaran in the race could have won the fastest navigation prize but, believing that Crowhurst was about to overtake her, pushed too hard and broke up.
- In sending the false reports Crowhurst showed real skill: he had to assess what the conditions were like in the area where he was 'sailing' and work out reasonable daily Distances Run.
- He also had to work the celestial navigation calculations backwards, from the answer he wanted to the fictitious readings. This was no mean feat.
- Robin Knox-Johnston (see above), who was the only finisher in the race, gave his winning purse to Crowhurst's widow.

The yacht *America*

In 1851 'the low black schooner' *America* sailed across the Atlantic and challenged the yachts of the Royal Yacht Squadron to a race in the Solent. No one took up the challenge but she was allowed to join in a race around the Isle of Wight. That race changed yachting history.

America was still anchored at the start so she was well behind on the first leg to the Nab Tower. However, she was so fast that she rapidly overtook the whole fleet down the back of the island. Queen Victoria was waiting at the finish in Cowes and asked someone with a telescope who was winning. He replied '*America* first, your majesty. There is no second.' *America* in fact beat the second boat by 18 minutes.

She was presented with the One Hundred Guinea Cup, later renamed The America's Cup, which has been raced for ever since and is the oldest international sporting trophy. The New York Yacht Club, as holders, defended the trophy 24 times in a row, the longest winning streak in the history of sports. They were finally defeated in 1983 by *Australia ll*, with her revolutionary winged keel.

After that first race *America* had a chequered career. Returning to America she was a blockade runner in the American Civil War, and a training ship at the US Naval Academy. Laid up ashore, a heavy snowfall fell on the roof of her shelter which collapsed, and she was crushed under the weight.

The yacht America

Key Bluffing Points

- The America's Cup had pride of place in the New York Yacht Club's model room for so long that, when asked what would be put in its place when somebody finally won it, the commodore replied, 'The skull of the guy who lost it.'

- For many years the NYYC insisted that challengers had to sail to America before racing. The seagoing challenger had little chance against the sleek home defender. (Perhaps this is fair, since *America* herself sailed across before that first race.)

- You have always had to be rich to take part in the America's Cup. During one defence the Kiwi team sold red socks to raise cash: almost everyone in the country was wearing them. Today, an America's Cup campaign costs well in excess of £100 million.

- A model of *America* has been tank tested and found to compare well even with today's designs. In other words, her 101ft hull was extremely slippery.

Ainslie

The most famous of all dinghy racers is Sir Ben Ainslie. He is the world's most successful Olympic sailor with a record of one silver and four gold medals for Team GB in consecutive Olympics.

Ainslie is a Jekyll and Hyde character: polite and modest off the water, ruthless on it. He never gives up and has an uncanny ability to come from behind:

- In the Atlanta Olympics his first race was a disaster.
- In Sydney he started the last race five points adrift.

- In Athens he was 9th in the first race and protested out of the second.
- In Beijing he contracted mumps three days before the regatta and finished 10th in the first race.
- In 2012 he had to have injections in his back and ankles before the regatta and was scoring poorly after the second day.

But his biggest comeback was in the 2013 America's Cup where Oracle Team USA were trailing the Kiwis by 1 race to their 8. After some modifications were made to the boat Ainslie joined the team as tactician and they won the next eight races in a row to take the Cup 9-8.

Ainslie sailed in the Laser class in his first two Olympics, where his chief rival was the Brazilian ace Robert Scheidt, who took gold in Atlanta. Four years later it all came down to the last race where Scheidt only had to finish in the top 21 to take the gold. Ainslie sailed him mercilessly down the fleet and *just* prevailed, Scheidt finishing 22nd.

His match racing tactics are now more common but in that race they were revolutionary, and Scheidt protested under the 'recognised principles of sportsmanship and fair play' rule. This was thrown out as no racing rule had been broken and Ainslie took the gold.

For the next three Olympics Ainslie switched from the Laser to the Finn dinghy, and went on to win three more gold medals in that class.

Key Bluffing Points
- All Ainslie's Olympic boats were called *Rita*. No one

knows why.

- After winning in Sydney, Ainslie received death threats from Scheidt's supporters, and effigies of him were burned in Sao Paulo. Apparently in Brazil sailing isn't a matter of life or death – it's much more important than that.
- The ideal weight for a Finn is 90-100kg. Ainslie is naturally 87kg, so it was double portions for him for years. At least it made a change from slimming for the Laser, where the ideal weight is 76-81kg.
- Both his Finn and his Laser are in the Maritime Museum in Falmouth. The chip out of the gold-medal-winning Laser's transom was caused by your author driving a photo boat into the back of this national icon while filming.

Ransome

Arthur Ransome is best known as the author of twelve children's books, the most famous of which, *Swallows and Amazons*, written in 1929, has inspired generations of children to take up sailing. It tells the adventures of John, Susan, Roger and Titty (please, behave) on their 14-foot lugsail dinghy *Swallow*. They sailed her to Wild Cat island, camped and did battle with the pirates Nancy and Peggy on *Amazon*. The lake and island are fictitious but reflect Ransome's time in the Lake District.

Ransome's own life was stranger than fiction. As the Russian correspondent of the *Manchester Guardian*, he may or may not have been a spy, or even a double agent. But he certainly played chess with Lenin and married Trotsky's secretary, Evgenia Shelepina, having first spirited her out of

Russia (and divorced his first wife). One of his adult books, *Racundra's Third Cruise*, describes their honeymoon sailing up the river Aa in Estonia in 1924. Evgenia was a formidable woman: over six feet tall, she slept with her pet snake on her chest.

Key Bluffing Points
- Ransome was a brilliant writer; it was said that he could even make a laundry list interesting.
- His philosophy and style are summed up beautifully by these lines on the building of his beloved *Racundra*:

  'I took a deep breath and signed the contract. This was among the few wise things I have done in my life, for, more than anything else, this boat helped me to get back to my proper trade of writing.'

  and

  'The desire to build a house is the tired wish of a man content thenceforward to a single anchorage. The desire to build a boat is the desire of youth, unwilling yet to accept the idea of a final resting place.'
- In *Racundra's First Cruise*, Ransome referred to Evgenia as 'the cook' because of the scandal it might have caused at the time if it be known that the already (unhappily) married Ransome was with an unmarried woman in a small boat.
- Despite her penchant for reptiles, Evgenia left their honeymoon cruise because there was a mouse on board.

GLOSSARY

Apparent wind: Not the result of a vindaloo, but the wind you experience when sailing (which could, of course, be the same thing).

Backstay: Sadly nothing to do with basques or corsets. The backstay stops the mast leaning forward. It also bends the mast, which flattens the mainsail.

Baggywrinkle: Rope which has been unravelled, then attached to the rigging. It stops the sails chafing, which can be painful. Also the area under the long-suffering skipper's eyes.

Bailer: A scoop to remove water from inside the boat. Also someone with sense who decides at the last minute not to go sailing.

Bear away: To alter course away from the wind. In this context nothing to do with naturism.

Beating: Don't go there. In this context it means sail to windward, in a series of zig-zags. At the end of each zig the boat tacks, turning through about 90 degrees.

Beaufort wind scale: A scale of wind speed with the associated effect on a yacht and her crew. E.g. Force 1: Light breeze, no waves, ok to go below and make a souffle. Force 10: Storm, very severe waves, best to struggle back to harbour and sell the boat.

Becalmed: In no wind, or what you might say to an anxious skipper.

Belly: The curve in a sail, or a sailor. You can reduce the sail's belly by pulling on the backstay and / or the vang. Sadly you don't get quite the same results with a corpulent crewmate.

Bight: An open loop in a rope or what you'd like to do to the skipper when he shouts at you.

Bilge: The space below the floorboards where bilgewater collects. More commonly the main constituent of the conversation of a bluffer.

Boat: A waterborne device for getting from A to B at 5mph and huge expense. For a boatbuilder, 'BOAT' is common parlance for 'Bung On Another Thousand'.

Broach: Either when the boat is out of control or what the skipper gives to his spouse to keep his marriage under control.

Broad reaching: Sailing downwind on a course between a reach and a run. In another context ladies should beware of it at the yacht club disco.

Centreboard: A foil which pivots down into the water to stop a dinghy drifting sideways. A daggerboard is similar but only moves vertically. A centreplate is not a denture, it's a heavy centreboard made of metal. Clear on this?

Channel 16: You might think this is a marine perfume, but in fact it's a) the VHF channel where you initiate a radio call and b) the emergency channel.

Cleat: Fitting designed to hold a rope under tension which can be known to jam just when you want to release the rope.

Clew: The lower, aft corner of a sail. When it rips be ready to quip 'Now we really haven't got a clew.'

Clove hitch: A useful knot for tying on the fenders. Also a shortage of spice in the galley.

Compass light: A light in the binnacle so you can see the compass at night. Also, the skipper's favourite fags, which smell even worse than his socks.

Compass rose: The markings on a traditional compass. Not to be confused with the barmaid at the Hope and Anchor, though she too has her points.

Cunningham: A rope that pulls down the front edge of a sail. The Americans call it a Sly Pig ('cunning ham'). Geddit?

Depression: Meteorological term for an area of low pressure or what the bluffer feels when his attempts to avoid the invitation onboard are unsuccessful.

Deviation: Occurs when the compass needle is deflected by lumps of iron in the boat (e.g. the engine) or a magnetic field (from the boat's electrics, the crews' mobiles, etc.). Also, the skipper's penchant for scantily clad…

Ensign: The flag at a boat's stern signifying her country of origin. It's fun to dip it to a warship, then watch them scurry about to dip theirs in return.

Flaked out: Before a rope or anchor chain is allowed to run it is flaked out on the deck in long S-shapes (to prevent kinks). Also a state of post-exertion for a crew member unaccustomed to physical activity.

Flashing: Navigational aids like buoys have lights that flash for identification at night. (E.g. Fl.R.5s is a red light which flashes every 5 seconds.) You can probably guess what else flashing describes, but it's not to be encouraged in the confines of a boat.

Forecabin: The cabin in the bow of a yacht. Sometimes where foreplay takes place.

Foul weather: Cold, windy and raining. Gives the bluffer the chance to say: 'I can't stand fair weather sailors, this is proper sailing.' This is usually just before you head below to the warmth of the saloon 'to check the bilge / chart / engine / see how the stew's doing…'

Gaff: A spar used to keep the top edge of a sail straight. Also, a nautical blunder. E.g. 'Hi, Skip. We had to switch off the echo sounder, it was beeping continuously…' Followed by 'CRUNCH!'

Genoa: A large foresail which extends aft of the mast. Also a large port in northern Italy. Gives the bluffer the opportunity to tell the world's oldest sailing joke: 'Genoa?' 'No, but I'd like to.'

Gimbal: A contrivance to keep a stove or compass horizontal when a yacht heels. Will also help the crew *gyre and gimble in the wabe* as they *beware the Jabberwocky*.

Gore-Tex: A waterproof, breathable fabric. Nothing to do with a native of Texas keen on carnage.

Gunwale: The join between the deck and the hull. Pronounced 'Gunnell' like 400m hurdler Sally, who would be a useful addition to anyone's deck.

Gybe: Picture a boat running downwind with the mainsail out on the starboard side. If the boat bears away the wind will get behind the sail and flick it across to the port side. The boat has gybed. It is an opportunity for everyone on board to duck or be knocked overboard.

Heads: The small compartment on a yacht housing a marine toilet and, often, a washbasin and shower. Two heads are better than one because you've then got some chance of abluting after breakfast.

Heel: When a boat leans over due to the pressure of the wind; also something you should not wear on the boat as it will damage the deck.

Imminent: Change in the weather within 6 hours in which time you were hoping to have had a shower and had a hot meal ashore.

In stays: Again, nothing to do with basques and corsets. When a sailing boat points straight into the wind and stops.

Jib: A small foresail occupying the space between the forestay and the mast. It ruins the tans of those sunbathing on the foredeck.

Latitude: The angular distance north or south of the Equator, measured along the vertical edge of a chart. Also, when the skipper allows the crew time off, probably to unblock the heads or change the engine oil.

Lift: When the wind frees. Or what you feel when you finally spot France after a channel crossing.

Luff: The front edge of a sail. Also, to alter course towards the wind. 'A luff' is the act of doing that, 'B luff' is what this book is all about.

Magnetic pole: The compass needle points to the magnetic pole, not to true north. The difference is variation. Also a nickname for a handsome Polish navigator.

MAYDAY! Forget cloggies and maypoles, this (from the French m'aider) is a serious request for help when a boat or person is in grave and imminent danger.

OCS: On Course Side means the boat is over the startline at the starting signal. She is then either disqualified or has to come back and start again. After which the language tends to be OCS (On the Coarse Side).

Off soundings: Very deep water (originally too deep to be measured by a lead line). Also unpleasant noises from the heads.

Over-canvassed: A boat carrying too much sail. Not to be confused with a bored member of the electorate.

PAN PAN Nothing to do with a marine lavatory. In fact it's an advisory VHF call to let people know you have a problem. If the problem gets worse, you send a MAYDAY (which might indeed prompt an urgent visit to the relevant facilities).

Pinch: You thought you knew, but it describes sailing too close to the wind, which is what you might be doing if you did it to a crewmate's bottom.

Quarter berth: A single bunk tucked under the cockpit. It's always a quarter the size needed to get any sleep.

Rake: The lothario in the crew or the angle the mast leans back.

Reaching: Sailing across the wind. Not to be confused with retching (although you will often do both at the same time, especially in a rough sea).

Reef: To reduce sail. Also a ring of coral or rocks in the sea around an island. The idea is to do the first, before you hit the second.

Reefer: A nautical blazer. Useful as a smoking jacket when you light up, ahem, a reefer.

Rhumb line: The direct line from A to B. In the Caribbean it's known as the Rum Line, the direct and quickest line to the bar.

Glossary

Running: Sailing downwind, i.e. away from the wind. Alternatively what you do when you first catch sight of the wreck of a boat your skipper has invited you to sail aboard.

Seacock: A tap which, when closed, blocks a pipe. This prevents the ingress of seawater. Also a chicken with a poor sense of direction.

Sheet: Not an exclamation of surprise, but a rope that pulls in a sail or lets it out.

Short-handed: A yacht with insufficient crew. (Often due to the skipper's tendency to shout, sulk, sail into rocks or belch continuously. And sometimes all four at once.)

Shroud: A wire that holds up the mast. Adjusting the shrouds and spreaders are crucial to tuning the rig. It's a complex process, forever shrouded in mystery to the average bluffer.

Sitting out (also called hiking): Moving outboard, with your feet under the toestraps, to keep a dinghy upright. After which you're knackered and may have to sit out at the club's disco.

Strong points: The bluffer should clip his safety harness to the yacht's strong points such as a shroud, backstay or jackstay. Once safely tethered he can enumerate his own strong points. If he can think of any...

Thwart: An attempt to prevent the boat from going to sea, or a transverse seat in a dinghy.

Trapeze: Gear to enable the crew of a dinghy to hang horizontally over the water with his feet on the gunwale. His weight counteracts the heeling effect of the wind, driving the boat forwards. Often leads to walking on water when he loses his footing.

Tumblehome: The narrowing of a yacht's hull as it nears the deck, i.e. the boat is widest halfway up the sides. Not to be confused with what the crew do after a good night ashore.

Twist: Your favourite dance move or the difference in the angle to the wind between the top and bottom of the sail.

Vang: The vang (or kicking strap) pulls down on the boom, forcing the mainsail into a proper wing shape. A vang that pushes the boom down is called a gnav.

Veer: The wind veers when it shifts in a clockwise direction. (When the wind shifts anticlockwise, it backs.)

Yacht: A hole in the water into which you pour money. Also a machine for creating cock-ups for the bluffer to resolve, thus honing his key attributes: nonchalance, inspired guesswork, and low cunning.